Broken Rainbows

Broken Rainbows

Growing Faith in a Changing World

G. Michael McCrossin

Sheed & Ward
Kansas City

Sheed & Ward™ is a service of The National Catholic Reporter Publishing Company.

Library of Congress Cataloguing-in-Publication Data
McCrossin, G. Michael, 1934-
    Broken rainbows : growing faith in a changing world / G. Michael McCrossin.
        p.   cm.
    Includes bibliographical references.
    ISBN: 1-55612-913-0 (alk. paper)
    1. McCrossin, G. Michael, 1934-   . 2. Spiritual life—Catholic Church. 3. Christian life—Catholic authors. 4. Catholics—United States—Biography. I. Title.
    BX4705.M4759A3   1997
    230—dc21   96-53402
                                                                      CIP

Published by: Sheed & Ward
                 115 E. Armour Blvd.
                 P.O. Box 419492
                 Kansas City, MO 64141-6492

To order, call: (800) 333-7373

Contents

To Kathleen,
Sean, Colin and Megan

Preface

. . . disconnecting from change does not recapture
the past. It loses the future.
    – Kathleen Norris, *Dakota: A Spiritual Geography*

This book began as a therapeutic exercise intended to
help me understand where I had come from, where I was
and, perhaps, where I was going. Many of the "self help"
books I have read had suggested writing a brief history of
significant moments in one's life as a way of coming to
grips with the past and resolving present tensions and
uncertainties. At first I resisted doing this, feeling that it
was both time consuming and unnecessary – it should be
possible just to sit down and think it through without
going through the writing. I found, however, that writing
not only helped to clarify my understanding of the past.
It also had a creative effect. The simple process of ordering
thoughts and putting them into words on paper assisted
in the development of approaches and ideas that helped
resolve the issues that rose into consciousness.

My central problem was that at the age of fifty-nine
I found my life adrift in an uncharted ocean. I had once
sailed in a well provisioned ship on an inland sea where
all the dangers were clearly located, the ports well marked
and both the start of the voyage and the end of the voyage
planned and documented. But now I seemed on a raft
nearly awash, without chart or even rudder, on an ocean

whose dangers were unknown, its boundaries forever beyond the horizon, with only a dim recollection of the
embarkation point and no clear idea at all of any goal.
The intricate web of images and words and systems of
thought that combined to make up the world view of the
first half of my life was forever shredded.

The need for a new world view remained, as did the
strongest intuition that the waters on which I floated had
a deeper sense and meaning. I felt that if I could only
enter into those waters more fully I could begin to see
the elements of a new view that would embrace all the
pieces of experience and would come together into a new
map of the world capable of sustaining my voyage into
the future on a much vaster body of water.

The first chapter of this book describes the world
view into which I was introduced at birth and to which I
clung for many years. It also describes the elements which
brought about the collapse of this world view as a map
for my own life. The second chapter attempts to set forth
the starting point for a new map and the qualities such
a map or world view would have if it were to be an effective
one, particularly the need for any new world view to take
into account and respect the underlying reality of my
original view, which was that of a western, Christian and
Roman Catholic individual living in 20th-century America.

The third through the seventh chapters suggest some
ways of understanding God and creation, sin, Scripture,
Jesus Christ, and our continuing relationship with God
and the community of those sharing the same faith experience. My intent and effort was to provide a set of ideas
that respected my fundamental faith experiences and also
respected the complex of ideas that arises out of modern
scientific thought and contemporary social and political
experience.

A final concluding postscript describes my reaction
to the preceding chapters and my thoughts on what the
future might hold. On the whole, I thought it just possible
that what I had produced was not a wild and aberrant

scheme. There might just be here a theory that could help satisfy our need to understand who we are and what it is all about at least for this stage in the development of the world.

* * * * *

Somewhere along the way of sorting out my thoughts and putting them on paper, it occurred to me that others might find some resonance with their own situation in these pages. I thought of a woman, a few years younger than myself but brought up in an equally rigid and all-encompassing Roman Catholic world, who drove around frantically every Sunday looking for a Mass that would be as short as possible (preferably one already begun but not so far into the ceremony that it didn't "count" for the Sunday obligation to attend Mass). She was well educated, working in one of the professions, and seemed to be getting little or nothing out of this exercise other than avoidance of guilt over an unfulfilled duty.

When I suggested she might better spend her time seeking something that opened her life to its depths, she looked wistful but said she couldn't because she wouldn't know how to explain this to her mother. Even though her mother had Alzheimer's disease and no longer recognized her daughter, the allegiance to the ways of childhood was too strong. But I had been there once, too, and I did not think that attitude would last her the rest of her life. She would join the many Roman Catholics I knew or read about who were questioning the beliefs of their youth and not finding adequate answers within the tradition.

In addition to other Roman Catholics, this description of search for a new world may also have some interest to Christians of other denominations, and indeed to anyone who shares in my desire for a world view that does not deny the reality of faith but also does not require that faith to be expressed only in terms and patterns that suited prior times while denying or overlooking much that is commonplace in the late 20th century. Finally, it may have some interest for those who have never experienced a living religious tradition, but who find the violence and materialism that ever more characterize the secular world banal and empty.

It is certainly possible that my own experiences and the thoughts to which they give rise are too unrelated to those of my contemporaries, whether coming out of the traditional Christian world or some other source. But I am convinced that some deep sea change is eroding the world view that has dominated the lives of so many, and that millions of people are waiting for a new world view, some of them actively seeking it, some simply standing by for the right moment to turn their eyes away from the old vision towards the new.

One reason for this is a highly unscientific survey of what is selling in the local bookstore. Not very long ago, books on religion and the category generically described as "self-help" would not have taken much space on bookstore shelves. If one assumes that the operators of bookstores are rational in their allocation of shelf space, one can only conclude that has changed and the aisles of books of this kind now on sale reflect the interests of the customers. If this is happening in the medium-sized city where I lived as I wrote much of this book, a place where national trends are customarily just a bit delayed, then how great must the ferment be in areas where a critical mass of discontent and seeking is more likely to have been reached?

In 1952 a female monkey living on an island where the principal food was sweet potatoes discovered that the gritty sand on the potatoes could be removed by washing the potatoes in a pool of water. The "invention" spread slowly, first to that monkey's offspring and then to others in a position to observe the process easily. Within a few years and a couple of generations, however, washing potatoes was commonplace to all the monkeys not only on the original discovery island but on other islands as well.

It is not clear whether the discovery was transmitted by migrating monkeys or whether it was independently discovered on the different islands. Whichever the case, it seems clear that the monkey population was ready for a new way of food handling and quickly adapted the procedure. The only resistance to innovation came from the adult males at the top of the monkey pecking order. Perhaps they preferred to eat sand with their potatoes rather than admit a female could find a better way!

Similar things happen in human communities. There is the obvious example of the sudden fall of the apparently unshakable Soviet monolith. To cite a much smaller but more personal example, when I was studying theology at the Jesuit seminary outside Baltimore we customarily wore black pants and a gray cotton jacket for most of our daily activities. None of us liked the outfits, but it was what had been worn by generations of Jesuits and would, it seemed, be worn so long as the Order existed. But one day somebody appeared in khaki trousers and a colorful sport shirt. Within a few months, the black pants and gray jackets had been largely abandoned and we suddenly looked just a little bit less like prison inmates and a bit more like a normal group of graduate students.

A time comes when a population is ready for a change. The old way has survived beyond its useful life and a suppressed but deep need for new forms of external expression arises. The urge for change grows until it can be no longer contained and then with astonishing suddenness bursts forth, like a tulip emerging from its dormant bulb with the appearance of the spring rains and sun, amazing in its brightness and life. It, too, will fade in time. But birth, death and new life are essential parts of the process of life and development. They cannot forever be suppressed, no matter how diligent the guardians of the old standards.

I am no longer surprised that those who are the leaders of the old world of thought and ideas are fierce in their resistance to change. Like the adult male monkeys, their strength and authority appears to come from continuation of the old order. It is hard to accept change when a lifetime has been devoted to a certain way of living, thinking and acting. And it is understandable that the old leaders would fear any change that would seem to call into question their authority and position. But King Canute could not stop the incoming flood of the tide, and neither can the leaders of yesterday's world stop a development whose time has come.

I think that time is upon us.

* * * * *

The ideas that are expressed in this book are not original. I cannot think of a single point that I have not seen either suggested or developed at some length in one or more of the many books dealing with science or religion or contemporary society or psychology which I have read over the past several decades. I did not, however, keep notes and it has been impossible to trace each idea to a particular writer or group of writers. Perhaps this has been fortunate since I did not, in any event, want to write a book that would look like an academic discussion of the ideas of other authors. So, with the exception of those few times when I have used a direct quotation from an author or referred to an author in the text, there are no references for the source of the ideas offered. There is, however, a bibliography which is offered both as a guide for further readings and also as a listing, partial at best, of sources. All quotations from the Christian Scriptures are from *The Oxford Annotated Bible* (Revised Standard Version, 1962).

At the same time as I insist that the ideas are not original, I want to insist equally on accepting the blame for any misunderstandings of what I have read, and also take the blame for the particular arrangement and configuration of ideas that come to light here. The basic experiences that I call faith experiences, as well as the recollection and description of my journey through expressions of that faith are, of course, unique to me – although I think that others may share similar faith experiences and may also have passed through the mental territory explored here on similar journeys.

* * * * *

Finally, I cannot conclude this preface without a statement of my gratitude to all the friends and relatives who encouraged and taught me along the way. I also want to thank Sheed & Ward for taking on my manuscript and especially its Editor-in-Chief Robert Heyer and my editor, Sarah Smiley.

CHAPTER ONE

Paradise Lost

What if earth
Be but the shadow of heaven, and things
  therein
Each to other like more than on earth is
  thought?
– J. Milton, Paradise Lost, V, 574

The mind is its own place, and in itself
Can make a heav'n of hell, a hell of
  heav'n.
– J. Milton, Paradise Lost, I, 253

It is late, close to midnight, on Holy Thursday in the spring of 1957. I and the other Jesuit novices are in the chapel attending a service called "Tenebrae" – "Darkness." The chapel is lit only by candles, and just dimly visible is the motto of the Order chiseled in gold letters in the Romanesque arch above the marble altar – "Ad Maiorem Dei Gloriam" – "To the Greater Glory of God." We chant psalms in Latin, the language of the Church throughout the world. Someone hiccups and a tremor passes through the back of the pew in front and the kneeler below. But it does not cause the ripple of shaking suppressed merriment common among the novices, high strung and nervous from the work of meditation and prayer. This is Holy Week and no time for laughter. The ebb and flow of the psalms washes over me, and I rest secure in the thought that this service is going on all over the world. The universal Church sharing in the trials of its suffering Savior and so making Him present for all.

We are joined with Christ in the Garden of Olives. Midnight approaches and darkness gains upon us as the candles are dimmed one by one until only a single light remains behind the altar. A rumbling crashing noise reverberates through the darkened chapel from the rapid hidden shaking of a great piece of tin. The final candle is extinguished and we are in total darkness. Lord Grey: "The lamps are going out all over Europe; we shall not see them lit again in our lifetime." Then and now they are going out in churches all over the world. And yet we know – did He? – that the lights will all come on again, brighter and more penetrating than ever in the Easter resurrection. I live in a timeless world of life and death and resurrection and life again.

The Holy Week liturgy was modified and 1957 was the last time Tenebrae took place at the novitiate chapel.

Wandering in the Garden of Eden

I have been a Roman Catholic priest, a lawyer, a teacher, a husband and a father. So, I know something, but not very much, about Christianity, philosophy, theology, law, education, marriage and parenthood. And in recent years I have been a reader of the works of Jung and Joseph Campbell, and books about Eastern religions, biology and physics. So I know something, but even less, about mythology, nonwestern religion, evolution and quantum physics.

Perhaps a little knowledge really is a dangerous thing. Perhaps if I knew more about any one thing it would dominate my mental world in such a way that other bits and pieces of knowledge could either be edged into insignificance or brought into a coherent whole. Or, perhaps, the desire for a coherent whole is simply a hangover from too much Greek philosophy and medieval theology. I certainly believe that my present is the sum of all my past, and a big part of that past has been a search for integrity and wholeness, expressible in some systematic way. Whatever its source, I know that I do have a deep down desire for the experience of living in one whole world where all the pieces are at home as well as for some coherent expression of that experience of wholeness.

The world into which I was born seemed coherent and whole for a long time. It was a world of regular church going on Sundays and holydays of obligation (often twice, what with Mass in the morning and Benediction in the evening). The one true God had revealed Himself once for all in Jesus Christ and his followers had formed the one, holy, catholic and universal Church to which I and my parents, all of my relatives and most of our friends belonged. Its teachings were infallibly true and covered the whole of human experience. What God had not revealed could be known by natural reason and, since God was the author of it all, there was and could not be any conflict between the truths of revelation and those discovered by human reason. If there appeared to be, it was simply because reason had taken a wrong turn, primarily because of human frailty and sinfulness. A careful attendance to the teachings of the Church would set things right.

My maternal grandmother had been a "convert." Raised as a Protestant (she never told me the denomination), after her marriage to my grandfather, a man out of a solidly Irish and Roman Catholic family, and the arrival of the first child, she had gone to the priest and taken "instructions." Only after their completion did she announce to the family that she intended to be a Catholic. She told me how hard it had been to overcome her fear. In her early childhood whenever she had to pass a Catholic church, she would start to run a block away and continue for at least a block on the other side, in terror that the priests or the nuns would kidnap her. Like other stories or evidences of Protestant views of Catholics, I took this as an example of the ignorance and benighted condition of those who believed ill of my church.

In due course it became evident that there were at least as many non-Catholics as there were Catholics. Part of my primary and secondary schooling was in public schools where "we" (the Catholics) were usually in a minority. We read from the Douay rather than the King James translation of the Bible when our time came at school prayer and we were given, sometimes a bit grudgingly, permission to arrive late on the first Friday of each month so that we could go to Mass and Communion. I, at least, felt that any inconvenience or smirks from my classmates were simply a part of the persecution that was to be expected by those who were fortunate enough to be in the true Church. Nonbelievers, we thought, were either guilty of a moral failure to accept the truth when offered or were "invincibly ignorant" – a kind of culturally induced innocent mental block that kept them from seeing the truth even when it was staring them in the face. And despite the teaching that there was no salvation outside the one true church, we were also taught that there was such a thing as baptism of desire for the good among the outsiders – if they truly desired to do the will of God that desire served as a baptism even though they might spend their entire lives in ignorance of the true church and the need to be actually baptized into it.

Except for the sermons, the church services were in Latin, a language I did not understand but was nonetheless moved by because I saw it as an example of the universality of the Church. Only later would we murmur that universal ignorance of Latin might be the shared experience. On a stand at home was a picture distributed by the Maryknoll Fathers, great missionaries to the Far East, showing Christ standing above the globe, with the message that at any hour the Latin Mass was being celebrated somewhere around the earth. That the vast majority of people in Asia and Africa had never heard of the Church was of no account. We prayed for the conversion of Chinese babies, went to see *Going My Way* and *The Keys of the Kingdom,* sang in honor of the Blessed Mother in her month of May ("O Mary we crown thee with roses today, Queen of the Angels, Queen of the May"), received holy cards for good grades and believed that the conversion of all was simply a matter of time. Years later, during the Korean War, a friend complained that he had often put a good portion of his allowance into collections for the conversion of Chinese babies – and "now, look what they are doing to us!"

Of course it wasn't all May crownings and holy cards. My earliest memory of attending church brings back Sunday Mass at the Catholic church in a small Pennsylvania town when I was three or a little over. I must have been talking or doing something wrong in church, because I remember my father taking me down the side aisle and outside to the car where I was spanked and then returned to the church, probably in a tearful but less deviant condition. And many of the church services in later years often seemed endless and boring (although the suspense of which one or more of we altarboys would faint during the lengthy Holy Thursday or Easter Vigil services sometimes countered that), not things I would have rushed to attend had it not been unquestioned that the entire family go and go often. But, on the whole, I think I felt this was a small price to pay for being a member of the one true Church, a citizen of a spiritual world that both embraced and overshadowed the ordinary world.

For reasons unknown other than that I had once passed through Hanover, New Hampshire and liked the looks of it, I wanted to go to college at Dartmouth. The word in return was "You can go anywhere you want so long as it's a Catholic school." So I went, not unwillingly, to Georgetown, then a small university in Washington, D.C., founded in 1789 by the Jesuits. It was the Eisenhower years, probably the last time in recent history that being an American made one feel almost as much embedded in a comfortable, coherent world as had membership in the Catholic Church.

Georgetown added scholastic philosophy and theology to my mental horizons and, along with the discovery of Gothic architecture, strengthened my experience of belonging to an ancient culture that embraced the whole of human experience. If I never quite embraced the notion of "the thirteenth, greatest of centuries," I was not far from it. God, man, nature, politics, art, science – they were all in bed together in a marvelously ordered world where feeling, reason and revelation were in harmony. Not surprising, then, that I entered the Society of Jesus a few months after graduation.

By 1956, my year of entry, the movement of young Catholic men and women into convents, seminaries and monasteries had reached its high water mark. The Neoscholastic movement in Roman Catholic thought, recovering the philosophical and theological traditions of the middle ages, had also blossomed. So I was plunged into a crowded, densely regulated and controlled world in which the great systems of thought of Thomas Aquinas and others rivaled the Gothic cathedrals in complexity and exuberance. It was all immensely satisfying, confirming my sense of belonging to a vast worldwide edifice containing space enough for anything and everything that humanity had or could devise. If it was a world not always in full accord with itself it was nonetheless one subject to and ultimately in accord with the laws of its creator. The only decision was to conform or not to conform. One choice led to peace, blessing, visions of God; the other to misery and damnation.

Recently, reading one of the Brother Cadfael mysteries written by the medieval historian Ellis Peters, I was vividly reminded of that early mental garden. The detective, a Crusader turned Benedictine monk and cloistered in a 12th-century English Benedictine monastery at Shrewsbury, is the keeper of a garden of herbs and the mixer and prescriber of an apothecary of herbal medicines. Town and monastery, citizen and monk live in a world where each respects the other, where each despite a difference in calling and daily life yet feels a common unity under a God whom they equally believe and fear. It all had such a familiar look, sound, taste, smell and feel, bringing me back with a sudden rush to a time when I, too, thought I inhabited a world that existed unchanged from the first through the 12th and on to the 20th century.

I believe now that I was fortunate to have once lived in such a world, and regret none of the time or effort spent working within it. At least, unlike so many I meet now, I know what it is to have a world in which to live. If that world moved away, becoming less a reality and more a dream, it nonetheless established a paradigm for any new world I might seek. Any such new world, however different its details from the old world, would have to express in its own way the integrity, wholeness and beauty of that Roman Catholic world of the first half of my life.

Leaks in the Boilerplate

The world where Gregorian chant drowned out the sounds of lesser melodies began to grow fainter years ago. Looking back, I detect at least four different paths leading away from the densely packed center of traditional Roman Catholic Christendom.

The first pathway started in the very center of the temple. During my thirteen years in the Jesuits, great changes occurred, arising in part from the Second Vatican Council in the early 1960s, in part from the sudden and precipitous drop in entries into the Order (as well as into all forms of Catholic institutional religious life) and perhaps most of all from the sudden decline that seems to finally overtake every imperial expansion, whether political, economic or religious. I and my contemporaries saw the way of life in which we had been trained disappear within a few years after our passage through it, like the wake of a ship suddenly coming to an end just a few yards behind the racing engines.

I think now that the Jesuits, true to their motto of being "in the world but not of the world," were moving to adapt to a different situation than that which prevailed at their 16th-century founding or even in the middle of the 20th century, when it might still have seemed possible that a vast network of defensive ramparts coupled with highly aggressive raids on opponents was the divinely ordered way for the City of God to meet the City of (fallen) Man. I was not, however, quite ready to see change as a necessity and at least a part of my decision to leave the Jesuits in 1969 was because I sensed with sadness the irrevocable breakdown of a world which, if increasingly seen as one with narrowing boundaries, was still an oasis.

During my studies in philosophy, a small group of us used to joke about the "truth vault" – that place deep beneath the seminary where the "truths" were stored, each brought out for a brief period to be shown to the students then lovingly restored to its safe place on the shelf. Those commissioned to enter the vault and bring out the truths selected for the daily lesson were warned to be careful "lest the truth escape." It was all a way of poking fun (gentle but then increasingly sardonic) at the very notion that we had a lock on truths eternal in nature, all the important ones already known and under control, our job being at most simply to keep them brightly polished, perhaps embellishing them here and there with an ornament that added to without distorting the clearly recognizable pattern, and occasionally presenting them to the believers like a mental Host in a mental monstrance.

Later during our studies in theology we changed the metaphor to account for the many different schools of thought that were accepted within the world of the church – Thomists, Suarezians, Scotists and all the other groups that disagreed among themselves as to a detail here, an approach there, but retained the essential mark of believing that the mind could abstract the essence of reality and encapsulate it in a logically related body of ideas that were eternally true. You could argue all you wanted, we said, as long as you were on the truth trolley. But woe unto those who stepped off and wanted to question the very existence of the trolley! With a faint but somehow growing hope we described those leaders of Neoscholasticism who were prominent at the Second Vatican Council as "the last of the madmen" – the final and perhaps fatal overreaching of that school which thought reality could be caught in its eternal essence within a human system of thought. Like the collapse of the Gothic cathedral at Beauvais, which had attempted to go higher than any other and had finally soared past the capacity of granite and human design, the medieval world of ideas appeared finally to be on the verge of collapse as a result of its efforts to freeze everything into a system eternally true and eternally unchanged and unchangeable.

Since I took my studies seriously and worked hard grappling with the intricacies of the scholastic systems I could not help noticing from time to time that the weather was getting stormy and the ship was springing a few leaks. From a distance it all looked solid as the *Titanic* just out of its builder's yard. Up close there were more than a few loose plates and rattling rivets, and the crew had to run constantly from one spot to another patching as it went. One professor explained that, at least as between the various accepted schools of theology, one could choose where the weak spots were and pick the ship most likely to complete the voyage. How that could be a possible course of action where we were striving for absolute truth was not clear, then or now. If faith needed a special ship to get from the shores of this world to the shores of the next, it seemed it should have something better than a rusty freighter.

Despite these problems, I remained for a long time convinced that my studies in theology, often said to be "faith seeking understanding," would bring me not to an intellectual overview of faith experiences but rather to an intellectualized faith, where the ideas were inseparable from the experience, in fact *were* the experience. Of faith as a deep relationship with God or persons or the rest of the world, I had little or no experience.

Once while I was sitting by the shore of Lake Michigan, several young men came by, wanting to talk about Christ in their lives. They said they had "met" Jesus. Curious, I asked them about the meeting, wanting to learn what had occurred, how it had felt. But they had nothing to add to the blank assertion that Jesus had "entered" their lives, and I was left with the thought that they had nothing more concrete than a strong intellectual conviction of being called to work for the kingdom of God, something I thought I already shared.

There were nonetheless incidents that someone more perceptive than I was might have seen as windows into a way of being and thinking which did not confuse ideas with the experience the ideas attempted to express. One in particular comes to mind. A fellow Jesuit was arguing strongly the need for maintaining some particular point significant in the theological system we were being taught – the distinction between "substance" and "accidents" I think. He claimed that one could not maintain the Real Presence (the true presence of Christ in the bread and wine consecrated during the Catholic Mass) without this distinction. It struck me strongly that this was complete nonsense, a turning of reality upside down. If one had an *experience* of the presence of Christ (which I even then must have instinctively seen as the true location of faith), then one's rating of the theological system of ideas would turn upon that system's ability to help in understanding the faith experience. Not the other way around! The inability of a particular system to explain a part of one's basic experience could not be the basis for overturning that experience.

Somehow, it entered my mind, I was living in a topsy-turvy world. I really believed in the traditional definition of theology as "faith seeking understanding," but here we were talking as if that underlying faith were dependent on the correct expression of an idea. The incident seemed minor at the time, but it was like a small crack in stone caused by the slow expansion and contraction of water. It would grow in time to shake the building where faith and understanding had somehow become indistinguishable.

The Barbarians Outside

The second pathway was that of growing experience with persons who did not share my world. For a long period family, church and educational institutions had largely protected me from encounters with those living outside my mental world of belief. Such people were encountered only as ideas to be examined and then identified and cataloged in the record book of "errors" rather than as actual human beings functioning quite successfully in worlds of perception, intuition and belief very different from that I inhabited.

The Jesuits sent me to the University of Chicago Divinity School to study for a doctorate in theology. I arrived in the summer of 1967. One of the first things I and an old Jesuit friend did was take a ride in the car, heading north from Chicago. The shock to my geographic idea of the United States on discovering that Milwaukee was only 90 miles north of Chicago was as nothing to the shock my worldview felt when I took a close look at the inhabitants of the University.

The Divinity School, started by the Baptists, had become a nondenominational school for the study of various aspects of religion. It was possible to concentrate one's studies in Christian Scripture, Christian Theology, History of Christianity, Ethics and Society, Religion and Literature or Comparative Religion. There were, by the time I entered, a fair number (but still a small minority) of students with a Roman Catholic background, and there were several Roman Catholics on the faculty. Despite its nondenominational character and multidenominational faculty and student body, the school was still recognizable as largely Protestant and its first major impact on me was its demonstration that these people could not be easily dismissed as invincibly ignorant. In many cases they were as familiar or more familiar with Roman Catholicism than I was, and yet they did not see any necessity to proclaim that Church as the one true one. Perhaps even more initially disquieting than their ideas was that so many of these people (and many of their colleagues in the other divisions of the University who were self-proclaimed atheists or agnostics) were so evidently thoughtful and good, even without the backing of the true faith. That was something I would have previously thought impossible or at best a freakish anomaly. I had instinctively thought of everyone outside as a kind of religious and moral barbarian. That response says a lot about how unseeing I was in my Roman Catholic Garden of Eden.

Best of all, Chicago was a place where ideas were taken very seriously. Ideas different from ones currently held were not simply "adversaries" to be automatically refuted. Instead they were thought about, discussed, walked around and considered with a refreshing freedom. No one was a heretic simply because he or she might promote an idea that seemed at variance with a tradition. In truth, traditions had rather hard going of it – something that said it was what had always and everywhere been thought or that it was an eternal truth was just a little bit suspect because of that very representation. There was certainly sympathy with the statement of Thomas Aquinas that authority was the weakest of arguments (a teaching of the great medieval theologian not stressed in my prior schooling)!

The freedom to look at experience and apply all kinds of ideas to it was exhilarating. For the first time I had to recognize that ideas were not necessarily coincident with experience, and that the experience could be retained while ideas were compared to it and accepted or rejected based on how well they illuminated that underlying experience. One day in class a student engaged a professor in a very heated argument on some point of Christian teaching. Both professor and student became more and more frustrated at not getting through to the other, as if they were coming at each other on parallel tracks that would never meet. Finally, like a bright light coming on, the professor said, "Hey, I think I'm finally understanding – you're not questioning my theology, you're questioning my faith." I remember a bright light coming on in my head, too. Whatever faith might mean, it did not necessarily lead to one fixed set of ideas.

When it came time to do my dissertation I shamelessly sought a subject that was limited in scope, did not require much knowledge of foreign languages and could be completed within a year. I had been much interested both in my seminary days and at the Divinity School in the writings of Teilhard de Chardin, a Jesuit paleontologist who had written, considerably to the distress of the official Church, several suggestive books on evolution and Christian belief. But to choose him as a subject would involve fluency in French as well as some serious knowledge of biology and archeology. So I chose to work instead on a group of nineteenth century American Protestant philosophers and theologians who had attempted to recast traditional Christian ideas in the context of an evolving world. It was one of those fortunate coincidences where not so reputable reasons for choice of a dissertation subject led to a critical development in my questioning.

My authors had made some considerable progress in applying Darwinian ideas to much of Christian thought. But, it seemed to me, they had stopped short of modifying their idea of God, who remained the distant, aloof yet in charge of it all and all knowing God that would probably have been acceptable to Calvin. (Once in discussing this with a Chicago professor we found ourselves in agreement that the God of Calvin, what with all His power and prescience, was a very believable God – but not one in whom either of us believed.) The dissertation was primarily an historical study of what my authors had said, and it was only as a critical afterthought that I was able to raise this neglect of God as a criticism of the completeness and value of their efforts. But the problem remained with me as a kind of faint but nagging headache. What kind of God might have made a world in which everything appeared to change and evolve? Would it be quite the same kind of God who was thought to have made the physical world exactly as it is now, never to change?

By the time I left the University at the end of 1970 I still thought of myself as a Roman Catholic (although I had left the Jesuits and the priesthood in 1969 and had married), but I did not feel the same constraint to conform my thoughts to the givens of the tradition. The Roman Catholic world was still there but it was looking more and more like a museum piece.

After leaving Chicago, the now rather dim intellectual world of my youth continued to be something of a presence, but what with raising three children and teaching, then working for a construction company started by my father, then going to law school and practicing first as a lawyer and later as a mediator of legal disputes, the need for living in a world as all-embracing as the one I had once known was for a time not very pressing.

However, in line with the Buddhist saying that when the student is ready the teacher appears, some 20 years after finishing at Chicago my wife and I both began to read books about Eastern religions, primarily Buddhism (and especially the Zen school) and Hinduism. We had also discovered the ideas of Joseph Campbell, first through a television series with Bill Moyers, then through his writings. None of this worked to convince us that our own Christian and Roman Catholic religious tradition was completely wrong. It did serve, however, to make us ever more aware that there were many religious traditions, all of them with a similar hold over their adherents and, what was far more important, all of them seeming to point towards a shared center of belief in the reality of a spiritual world that interpenetrated the everyday world. Obviously the religious traditions differed greatly in their emphases and in their ways of explanation and thought. But I felt strongly that the similarities were far greater than the differences. All of this was through reading. I had not as yet had any direct experience of another religion.

That changed in 1992 with a visit to an Indian woman living in a highly unlikely place – a tiny German farming village about 40 miles from Frankfurt. We had read about her in a book by Andrew Harvey, *Hidden Journey*, and felt strongly moved to see for ourselves. We found Mother Meera, said to be an incarnation of the divine mother, a quiet, gently smiling, youngish woman, giving darshan in a room holding 60 or 70 people. Unlike the elaborate liturgies of our experience, darshan was a very simple ceremony in which one came forward and knelt in front of the seated Mother Meera. After giving each other the traditional Hindu salutation with joined palms and a short bow ("the god in me greets the god in you"), Mother Meera placed her hands on my head for about 30 seconds, then we looked directly into each other's eyes for a similar period. No words, no other movements. Just a return to one's seat while others went up.

Harvey's book talked about seeing light emanating from Mother Meera's head. I don't know what I expected or hoped for, but nothing special occurred during the time her hands were on my head or while I looked deep into her eyes. Afterwards I felt as if my head were slowly expanding to fill the room, so much so that I thought for a moment I would bump into the ceiling. But it was not anything overwhelming, just a gentle feeling of slow expansion. In recollection I am inclined to think that is exactly what it was – my mind *was* expanding with this different form of religious experience. I could no longer be held by any conviction that only one religion was true and all others were false.

Shadows and Pools

The third pathway was, and is, that of self analysis and self knowledge. As the poet said, "Human kind cannot bear very much reality" (T. S. Eliot, *Burnt Norton*, I). Not very regardful of our discomfort, reality keeps banging at the door and occasionally breaks in. It broke in for me in October, 1987, at a meeting for cancer patients and their "support" persons held at a camp normally used for religious meetings in a canyon running down to the Pacific Ocean near Malibu. A malignant lump had been discovered in my wife's left breast in late 1985, then in the other breast a year later. They were small, surgically removed, the area treated with radiation, and prospects were good. But it had moved first her and then me to look into the relationship between cancer and the whole of our lives and we had traveled to attend one of the week-long meetings of the Simonton Cancer Center.

The weather was not particularly good and the Los Angeles smog not entirely absent. But the camp was in a grove of eucalyptus trees and the site had once been an American Indian healing ground. Hot and dusty, it nonetheless radiated a peace in the midst of the Los Angeles sprawl, conducive to taking a hard look at where we were in our lives. And the meetings, with the opportunity to talk of our experience and hear the experiences of others, coupled with time to meditate, ate slowly into the walls of denial and reserve built over the years. On the next to last night we – my wife and I and her two sisters, one my wife's twin who also was being treated for breast cancer – went out to dinner. As usual I had too much to drink, became angry and argumentative and spoiled the evening for everyone. After a miserable night I met at breakfast with one of the conference leaders and was able, for the first time, to say in the next public meeting that a large part of my and my wife's problems and issues was due to my being an alcoholic.

It was the start of a new direction which led to encounter groups, counseling, and much reading and discussion in an ongoing effort to visit my childhood, make peace with my parents, acknowledge mistakes and wrong turnings and perhaps, most of all, recognize that I was not the bad person that, buried inside the shell of outer confidence, I had feared myself to be for as long as I could remember. I'm still working on it. In part writing this book came out of a need to better understand where I have been and where I am going.

There are still shadows there that frighten me, things I am not sure I have been able to acknowledge. And occasionally that familiar wave of anger starting deep in the lower stomach moves up through my chest and into my head and I feel myself drowning once again. But it has grown less and I take that as encouraging. And I have found myself growing closer to my wife (after nearly 25 years of at best an armed neutrality) and my children, whom I very nearly lost forever. All because of my rages and efforts to control their lives as I had tried to control my own. It had been a hopeless effort to obtain peace and security through meeting demands I once thought were imposed by others but in fact had been set upon myself by myself.

I grew up an only child in a family of good, well-intentioned and intelligent parents who had themselves been raised in families where alcoholism, Victorian morality and the lace curtain variety of Irish Americanism had combined into a lethal brew. The great question of my years at home was "What would the neighbors think?" The worst reproach was that someone "did not know how to act," as if there were only one right way to act in any situation, apparently known by intuition to all good children. I thought I didn't care about what the neighbors thought and wanted only to act as myself – and felt all the more guilty because of these wayward ideas. I concluded that safety was to be sought in thinking everything out ahead of time and then attempting to control every aspect of any situation that arose. Of course it didn't work – and again I felt guilty because I had not been able to accomplish what was in fact an impossible effort.

I spent as much time as possible with a grandmother. She took me to the movies, bought me sundaes, talked to me at length about anything and everything, entrusted me with the great task of painting her attic and, in general made me feel good, special and loved. I can remember every room and nearly every piece of furniture in my grandmother's house, but I recall very little of the many apartments in which I lived with my parents. She may have saved my life.

And yet that was not all there was to it. For, along with the intelligence and curiosity and dissatisfaction with the ways things were, there must also have been love in my parents, however hard a time I had in recognizing it or remembering it. A note recently discovered, written by my mother and sent with a birthday present in 1970 a few months after I left the Jesuits: "The whole wide world would not be enough for us to give you, if we were telling you how much you mean to us! So, will be content with telling you we love you and your happiness is our happiness even as your sorrows are our sorrows." Perhaps, finally, the peace can descend with acceptance that they did the best they possibly could. That is all I can really expect in a real world, however much I might have wanted more from an ideal world. But I remain unsettled. Is it true that to understand all is to forgive all? I hope it is.

I know now that my love for the Church was at least in part a transferred hope of love in return. Mother Church, however, was then (and now) more into sin, guilt, repentance and control by authority than it was into love or healing. At the height of enthusiasm for the reforms of the Second Vatican Council, which emphasized that the work of the clergy was service to the church community, our local monsignor confided to me that he could not agree more – and his service was to tell people what to think and how to act. It is hard to change old habits and the years since the Council have been ones of regression by the official Church.

Recovery is a slow process and there are still many minutes, hours and days when a bleak sense of worthlessness settles in like a black mist over a bog. But there are more often days when expectation rises and the way forward looks pregnant with both purpose and surprise. I am on a journey down a road I do not yet know, towards a goal not yet even an outline but already held in an aura of excitement and promise. I have seen pictures of cenotes, those deep, sinkholes in the Yucatan where the Maya sacrificed treasure and perhaps their people. A recurring image is of plunging headlong into the cool waters and swimming ever deeper in search of what may finally be found at the bottom of the waters, where springs feed the pool. I do not think I will find death unless it be a death that is entry into life.

Tantum Quantum

The fourth pathway was a renewed interest in science. I had entered college intending to go on to medical school and had taken a series of courses in physics, biology and chemistry during my freshman and the first semester of sophomore year. But after changing to the arts program and a major in English literature, I had not so much as looked at a book on science until a few years ago. I was able to ignore the issues raised by contemporary scientific ideas of the world for a worldview in which all the present was substantially and immutably established at the time of creation.

One of my children is a student at the University of Notre Dame. A recent issue of the University's magazine carried an article about Notre Dame's concerns and efforts to retain its character as a Roman Catholic institution of higher learning. If there was any solution, the favored one seemed to be assuring that new faculty would have a strong commitment to the Catholic tradition as well as excellent academic credentials. It appeared this might work in various fields loosely described as the "humanities." Those in the natural sciences thought they would have a problem. There were very few people choosing to study in the natural sciences who had strong traditional religious commitments. If you had a passion for the one, you were not likely to pay more than a passing nod to the other.

It is easy to be sympathetic to those who look out on the world and see evidence of design and obedience to "natural" laws ultimately originating in the mind of a divine creator. Just as it appeared to most prior to Copernicus and Galileo that the sun circled the earth, so it is easiest to agree with Einstein that "God does not throw dice." Those who say or think otherwise must be very strange birds indeed, perverse, perhaps with some primitive grudge against God and order. Not the kind of people good religious folk would want to associate with.

Christianity, although its credibility was a bit damaged by early condemnations of the heliocentric theory, was able to enter into a four-century-long peace with the scientists so long as it was Newtonian science. God was not required to make daily adjustments to keep everything running smoothly, as an earlier piety had believed. But the uniformity of Newton's laws, their character of applying at all times and places, seemed a ready parallel to the tradition's proclamation of the universality of natural law. If Laplace could tell Napoleon his system had no need of the hypothesis of God, educated people, unless of the village atheist variety, could still believe that a creator God had set it all in place, with an established divine order and plan that was now found manifest in the laws of thermodynamics. The accepted solution was benign neglect: to allow the Church its freedom to pursue spiritual matters, while science pursued the makeup and manipulation of the material world. The best of all possible worlds!

Science did not stand still, and the tenuous peace unraveled as new discoveries challenged the traditional view of the world. Darwin took his voyage in the *Beagle* and theorized about evolution and the development of species. Astronomers found ever more distant stars and, with the determination of the speed of light, concluded that the universe was far, far older than the Biblical story implied – billions of years old with, in the worlds of Carl Sagan televised to millions, "billions and billions of stars." This vastness provided the necessary time for evolution to have occurred – all the minute changes in configurations of atoms and molecules and organisms in response to opportunities for better adaptation for survival that eventually led to the existence of human beings, so late in the day that humanity's time in relation to the whole is as the final inch below the ceiling of the top floor in a hundred story building. If we are indeed created in the image of God, it was not at the start but only after an almost incredibly long development. What was happening to the traditional story of creation?

Less dramatic for most than evolution and its all but infinite time and space but at least as destructive to the traditional world view was Einstein's relativity. Newton's universe assumed a single point of view on the world, with time and space uniformly the same throughout the universe. Relativity says there is no single point of view and that time and space are dependent on the movement of the measurer relative to that of the thing being measured. It is the familiar but hitherto overlooked phenomenon of sitting in a train stopped at a station, and looking at a train in an adjoining track. One begins to move – but am I moving or is the other train moving? My senses may tell me that I am, even though I may not be. That one, by application of all the senses, can usually be sorted out correctly. Yet we know that the earth moves, although none of our senses indicates that, in fact to the contrary. Here we stand or move, with no fixed point of view, no absolute time and space. What could God have been thinking about to create such a world?

Then there is quantum reality. Stranger and stranger still, at the very innermost heart of apparent surface stability, the elements of the universe come and go in chunks or waves, surfing in and out of actuality, their state at any given moment dependent on an observer seeking to determine their indeterminate evanescence. Prior to understanding reality in quantum terms, it had been argued whether light was a stream of particles or had the nature of a wave. It seemed that it must be one or the other, although it appeared in different experiments to exhibit sometimes one aspect, sometimes the other. Central to the quantum world is the discovery that light is both particle and wave and, much more interesting, that the two conditions are superimposed on one another so that at a given moment light is both a particle and a wave or (alternatively) is neither a particle nor a wave. Only at the moment of a particular observation (the nature of which is chosen by the observer) does this state of superimposition "collapse," so that light appears in that particular experiment as a wave or as a particle.

Schrodinger's famous cat, a thought problem designed to capture for the human imagination the way the quantum world operates, helps us to comprehend what the physicists are claiming. Imagine a cat in a closed box together with a quantity of poison that can kill the cat and that may (or may not) be released depending on whether a radioactive particle from a source within the box strikes a detector in the box. The detector is switched on just long enough so that there is a 50-50 chance of an emission from the radioactive material. Is the cat dead or alive? When we open the box we will know whether it is dead or alive at the moment of opening. In the strange world of quantum phenomenon, however, the cat is neither dead nor alive (or is *both* dead and alive) until the box is opened, at which point the two possibilities collapse into one actual living or dead cat. In the real world of

cats our commonsense insists that the cat, if it is found
dead when the box is opened, actually died at some moment prior to the opening of the box at the time an
emission from the radioactive material struck the detector.
But this is a quantum cat designed to show us how the
world operates at its most fundamental level – and there,
contrary to all our normal expectations, there is a fundamental indeterminacy that is not resolved into straight-
forward and "normal" actuality until there is an
observation event. From the standpoint of the fundamental distinction in both the traditional religious worldview
and the scientific worldview prior to quantum reality, the
most startling conclusion arising from the new physics is
that the sharp distinction between subject and object,
between subjective musings and objective truth, was forever blurred and even destroyed.

Whether this makes sense or not, it is the world of
quantum physics and a successful one, leading to television sets and lasers and other commonplaces. So I found
myself unable to ignore it, found myself also charmed by
ideas about action at a distance, the "awareness" of atoms,
complexity and chaos and a world always striving and
succeeding to live "on the edge" between chaos and in-
ertness. Whatever was going on, it did not look like the
first century or thirteenth or nineteenth century view of
the world. Where were the armies of unalterable law?
Where the plan and the grand design?

*   *   *   *   *

If I have learned anything, I have learned that there are
no general answers, no eternal ways of acting and being
that must be always and everywhere the same regardless
of the individual person's situation. I, like everyone else,
have my own particular history, my own angels and devils,
with which only I can deal and only in a way that respects
through discerning eyes my past, my present and whatever
future there still remains. Life is the discovery of one's

own path, made as each step is planted. Like the knights of the round table going out to seek the Holy Grail, each of us must enter the forest by our very own path.

Life is a great voyage of discovery, one in which we must take the risk of venturing into those regions where the maps tell us monsters lie. We cannot know otherwise if there are really monsters or instead the angels of our beginning transformed into new sharers of evolving life.

CHAPTER TWO

Marching, Marching

I hear it in the deep heart's core.
 – W. B. Yeats, "The Lake Isle of Innisfree," st. 3

Truth *happens* to an idea. It *becomes* true, is *made* true
by events. Its verity *is* in fact an event, a process: the
process namely of its verifying itself, its veri-*fication*.
Its validity is the process of its valid-*ation*.
 – William James, *Pragmatism*

It is more important that a proposition be interesting
than that it be true.
 – Alfred North Whitehead, *Adventures of Ideas*)

Do I dare to eat a peach?
 – T. S. Eliot, "The Love Song of J. Alfred Prufrock"

*I am on the covered rear patio area of the house, sitting on a
spring steel chair, a relic of the 1930s acquired from the owners
of the first house we bought. The seat and back cushions have
been often recovered, the chair itself, prone to rust, repainted so
often that its once clearly defined corners now have soft curved
surfaces, like fingernails with too much thick nail polish. But it
is enormously comfortable and the spring steel form moves slowly
up and down, a bob in a pool of air responding to every small
tug of my body.*

The river gravel aggregate of the floor is dark sand colored, spreading out past the thin columns supporting the second story verandah, beyond what was once a small fish pond, now a gravel filled depository for a recirculating fountain and potted plants. Its edge joins the white concrete deck surrounding the kidney-shaped pool, the decking curiously etched as if by large drops of acid fallen from the sky. The pool mirrors the light blue of the sky. Overhead a wind chime tinkles intermittently, the breeze mostly too soft to stir its pipes. A bird calls then flies out of the live oak tree towards the distant fairway, perhaps stirred by the soft yet high-pitched drone of an approaching golf cart. The scene is filled with bushes and flowering plants, their names all known to my wife but mostly unknown to me.

Sitting in the protecting chair my eyes lose focus and the scene is flattened, loses its depth dimension, patterns itself like a painting created before the discovery of perspective, and I find the barriers between myself and the plants and the pool and the bird dissolving. The single note of a chime is frozen and motion ceases; time disappears and only the present in which I am fused to my surroundings is real. I am neither an isolated individual nor fully merged. It is a unity in which the barest consciousness of distinction remains but with no sharp difference, as if I and all that surrounds me are largely dissolved into an underlying single reality. We are one more than we are many, our common ground flowing through all our edges. From somewhere in the abyss of consciousness a surge of warmth wells up and the intuition surfaces that this unity extends beyond everything present, endless, timeless, a source of all that pervades all without sharp distinction. It is benign, peaceful beyond understanding.

Later it occurs that this experience is the closest I have come to God. And yet the use of that term God is discomforting. My imagination is tied to a gigantic white-bearded father, to a demanding giver of laws and an exact accountant of the credits and liabilities of the conscious products of creation, to some One who is, if anything, completely other. What does an experience of the immediate relation of all reality have to do with that? Does it mock all that I have been taught in other times and places?

Trial and Error

In 1992 my older son called from Paris where he was working as a night clerk in a hotel on the Left Bank. He had been watching a local television program and had seen a report about the Bishop of Corpus Christi, the Texas city where we lived. The Bishop was in the process of excommunicating several Roman Catholics who worked at abortion clinics and his actions stood out enough in the Catholic Church's campaign against abortion to make national and even international news.

By that time my wife and I had grown sufficiently distant from the beliefs of our youth (she came from a background very similar to mine) that we felt ourselves more outside than inside the battle within the Catholic Church over abortion. We were in fact then attending a small Episcopal church in Corpus Christi that we had heard about while at a conference for business and professional people held in the hill country northwest of San Antonio. Fifteen years earlier we had visited an Episcopal church in Nashville while I was in law school and given some thought to joining it. But our attachment to Roman Catholicism and the prohibitions that we had heard so often in our youth against even putting a foot inside the door of a Protestant church were still too strong. They kept us from anything more than a wistful glance.

By 1992 we were actively seeking a religious community where the center of attraction was something more than who could get out of the parking lot quickest after Sunday Mass. We were ready to try a different way of being Christian. And so we went to the newly built church only a few blocks away from our home, expecting we knew not what but hopeful. The service, so very like the Roman Catholic Mass, with just enough minor changes in the language and the order of the ceremony to make us pay attention to the Book of Common Prayer, was familiar and reassuring. What was new was the spirit in the congregation – people talked to each other, embraced, sang with real volume and gave every sign of a group that cared deeply about its members. It was the same and yet entirely different from our past experience of church ceremony. For perhaps the first time we had a sense that spirit was present and that being a Christian did not mean catching only faint glimpses of a light from the distant past.

We plunged in as into a pool after the desert. I moderated a group studying the scriptures; my wife was one of several parents who set up and ran the religious education program for the younger members of the church. The ability of the Episcopal Church to tolerate a considerable variety of philosophical and theological points of view was soothing balm after all the "you can't say that" and "you must think this" of the past.

Gradually, however, we sensed that we had not yet found a home. With evangelical enthusiasm our congregation was intent in adding new members and raising new buildings to accommodate them. There was a sense that the church – its physical buildings and plot of land – was the center of religious life and that our goal was to be a place of refuge from the rest of the world. The day we talked seriously about building a gymnasium so we could play basketball with other members of the congregation was the day I finally had to question whether I wanted to be part of an enterprise that I felt was still looking inward rather than outward, that was trying to set up a community separate from the world rather than a be part of the world.

And then there was a growing problem with the range of permissible ideas. I found myself unwilling and unable to say things in our study group, fearing to offend the views of those who had traditional understandings of Christianity. One Sunday, trying to offer some thoughts about the presence of God in the world and the relationship between man and God, I was challenged by a concern about pantheism, coming from a woman whose disturbance and even fear was writ large on her face. I wanted a place to explore new ways of expressing the Christian faith but I didn't want to upset those not ready to take new paths. I was too uncomfortable myself to stand being the source of discomfort to others.

I tried for a while to find something satisfying in the writings of contemporary Christian theologians, particularly those who had taken a look at modern science and tried to show there was no conflict between the Christian tradition and that scientific understanding. But it all sounded like the efforts of the old astronomers trying to tickle the earth centered system of Ptolemy so it could explain the increasing number of observations that were not easily incorporated into a system of perfect spheres encircling the earth. If you added enough epicycles, each itself a perfect circle, you might just be able to "explain" the observations and, if so, you could successfully predict at least some events. But it was appallingly cumbersome and the whole apparatus cried out for simplification. It was as if you wanted to go from Manhattan to Brooklyn and were routed over the moon, around Mars and back to earth. Somebody needed to build a Brooklyn Bridge!

Eastern religions, about which I read much but had little direct experience, offered another possible way of thinking about my experience. But there were theological disputes there, too, and although the emphasis was much more on experiencing the underlying unity of all things than on the dogmatic expression of the nature of that unity, the quarrels between the various schools of meditative practice seemed as complicated as anything Christian theology had produced. More problematic still was the denial it might require of what seemed to me best about the Western tradition – the importance of each individual, the notion of forward movement in history rather than a circular and endless turn and return of the wheel of time, the desire not simply to empty the mind (which Christian mystics shared with those from the East) but also to fill it with ideas and systems that might aid in a deeper experience of the depths of reality. If nothing else, I was sympathetic to the view of Augustine that we talked about God not in order to contain in our understanding what was beyond our understanding, but in order to avoid silence. We are related to each other as well as to the underlying unity and, although there is a deepest level at which ideas are not only useless but harmful, there is also a level on which ideas must be called into existence and cultivated.

Then there was always the temptation of secular humanism – looking solely at the world around us and at human beings in particular to find answers to the mystery of being, who we are and where we are going. But freedom from the gods of yesteryear had not brought any exaltation of spirit after the initial exhilaration of shedding a burden had passed. Materialism, consumerism and greed looked like the winners. I thought it likely that the final resting place of the environmental movement might well be in the cost effective grave of accounting rather than in any new and satisfying vision of the relationship between all that could be perceived and all that I now intuitively felt underlay the surface of things.

It was finally time to look for a new way of thinking that denied neither the past nor the present, that would embrace all facets of my experience.

Some Preliminaries

The effort spent on trial and error was not a waste of time. It helped in sorting out the issues facing me. Where were the real points of stress? What out of my past was good and worth keeping? What needed to be discarded? Where should I seek renewal? I had to work my way through a forest before getting to the foot of the right mountain. By the middle of 1994 I felt I was finally at a real starting point. Before beginning the climb, however, I needed to spell out some preliminaries. It was time to sort out tools, make sure I had the right things in my backpack in order to assure survival on the coming slopes and a chance of reaching the top. Like all packing for a trip, this effort could be tedious. But there was no avoiding the preparatory work. It reminded me of the old Army instructor's list of how to teach recruits: First, tell them what you are going to tell them, then tell them, then tell them what you told them. I would be both instructor and recruit.

1. It's All Autobiographical

Augustine's *Confessions* is a classic model of the autobiographical approach to stating Christian beliefs, as have been the works of many a Christian mystic. The writings of contemporary thinkers taking an existentialist approach have also relied heavily on autobiographical details. But by and large Christian thought has been oppressively objective, as if some unwritten law stated "thou shalt not refer to personal experience." Like the talk of sex and politics banished from the Victorian dinner table, it has seemed a theological gaffe to talk about one's own faith experience as the starting point for any explanation. The complete avoidance of "I" and reliance upon learned footnotes referencing the equally nonsubjective works of other writers has been the customary correct mode of writing.

My experience denied that approach. I had come through a period of recognizing that systems imposed from without, built upon authority, however learned, did not respond to either my faith or my search for answers. So if I was going to get anywhere at all, it would have to be by using my experiences, my history to discern what answers there might be.

But it had to be all of my experience, the bad as well as the good. Someone once said that we don't learn from experience, we learn from bad experience. It would not do just to plunge into the best and throw out everything disturbing, displeasing or contradictory. This something called myself was a whole jumble of experiences, none of which could be discarded. I might find my child-

hood lacking in love or support, but that didn't permit
me to deny the existence of my parents or the good they
had given along with the bad. I couldn't go back to the
starting point, take that infant by the hand and bring him
to a new life. What I might be able to do is understand
what happened and build upon that understanding towards a new set of ideas and beliefs that brought everything into a new framework and did not leave anything I
could recollect outside the picture.

2. Babies and Bath Water

An occupational disease inflicting those who would
try to do something new is reinventing the wheel. Instead
of attempting to develop a new understanding of the
Christian tradition I had already experienced, I might
have attempted the construction of a world view different
in every respect from anything with which I was familiar,
all in an effort to avoid contamination by any aspect of
that familiar form. But, like the aged Notre Dame priest
in the movie *Rudy*, I had learned two things: there is a
God and I am not God. Assuming God existed, it was
God's job to initiate a completely new religious world if
it were ever needed. And if God didn't exist, then any
effort of mine to invent a new religious world would be
an exercise in futility.

So a second preliminary decision was to build on
such traditional Christian terms as God, Jesus, the Fall,
and Creation. I suppose I might have started with the
Void or the Great Spirit or Buddha or Mohammed, but
why attempt to unpack a tradition with which I had little
familiarity when there was one ready to hand that was
very familiar? If my journey was to provide the source
material, then I had no choice but to work with what I
had been given.

The obvious problem with using traditional images
or ideas or terms is that they come densely packed with
accumulated history – in the case of the Christian terms,

nearly two millennia of baggage. God was not just a word pointing to the center of reality, it was a word stuffed full of philosophical and theological bits laboriously woven into a complex idea over the centuries. And Jesus was not just the name of a man from Nazareth met this morning outside the temple, someone about whom we as yet knew hardly anything. Now it was the name pointing to a complex of understandings and interpretations first initiated by his early followers and then expanded down through time by generations of believers.

I wanted to see if there was a different way of understanding God and Jesus and Creation than what had been handed to me as a child and then a seminarian. That would require removing at least a sizable portion of the traditional content and replacing it with something else. At the same time I didn't want to lose the traditional container. It was the classic problem of throwing out the baby with the bath water. The bath water I was eager to see flow down the drain. The baby I wanted preserved.

I recalled the words of a former law partner. Asked whether he ever returned to the town where he had been born, he answered: "I go often, to visit the tombs of my ancestors and to congratulate myself on my wisdom in leaving." I've left my home town, but the tombs of my ancestors are still there, and they deserve visiting and respect.

3. Facts – the Thing's Just There

I used to think I understood what Sergeant Friday wanted when he said, at least once a week on *Dragnet*, "Just the facts, ma'am." But I'm no longer so certain. The facts seem increasingly elusive; they come and go and change. I'm like my dog. She sits patiently by my chair at dinnertime every evening. If I have not given her something to eat within a few minutes of starting the meal, she whines, first softly then with increasing urgency. Memories of "Don't feed the dog at table" echo in my mind and, perhaps because of that, I don't resist passing a scrap from my plate to her mouth. This has happened countless times. But she has an instinct not to act too suddenly. What is offered must be inspected carefully, sniffed at, perhaps a tentative touch with her tongue. Peas and carrots are not food in her world. Bread and meat and potatoes are. Once assured that food is being offered, she takes the bite. There is no hesitation when a second piece of the same thing is offered, and I must drop it quickly into her open mouth or risk the chance of small teeth catching a finger. Food is a fact in her world only when it has been carefully checked.

I do not remember crawling across the floor as an infant. But I have watched my own children starting to learn. They are interested in everything, touching each item, putting it in their mouths if possible. They hold it, look at it as if memorizing the shape and contours, then set it down, curiosity satisfied for the moment and go on to something else. Is this how we begin to separate the things outside ourselves from each other and from our own selves? A world of facts begins to take shape. All the things that are not me, but that I dependably find each morning as I get up and start another day. First my mother and my father, then my crib and the stairs and the doors and windows. Then grass and dirt and the hard pavement. On to other houses and people and the street and, when I am allowed outside after dark, the moon and stars, the wind whistling among the trees.

How much education and experience we have determines the extent of the facts that our minds recognize. Some, perhaps a majority of the facts accepted in a developed and complicated civilization were once theories. Over time the theories have been found to fit accepted facts so well that the theory itself becomes a fact. That table looks solid, unmoving. But if you have studied physics you are likely to recognize as a fact that beneath all that apparent solidity are nuclei and electrons (and other particles if you are up on the current research) in constant movement through empty space much vaster than the particles, all held together by a variety of forces unseen other than by their effects.

A better and more widespread example: we take it as a fact that the seemingly motionless earth on which we stand spins daily about its axis and revolves annually around that sun which persistently appears to our senses to be the only thing moving. We learned that several centuries ago and what would once have been thought a crazy notion is now accepted by all. (Or by mostly all. I recall coming down to breakfast at a Jesuit residence the morning after NASA placed a space vehicle in orbit around the earth. One of the fathers was in denial and kept repeating "What goes up must come down." We thought he was joking but finally came to accept that we might be dealing with the last believer in the preCopernican universe.)

It is also a fact that facts cease to be such. It is not a fact that the world stands still and the sun moves. Instead I learn that just the reverse is the real state of facts. If I could still have had any doubt, then it is finally banished as I stand on top of a mountain in Yellowstone Park in 1969, looking at the moon above and at a small black and white screen on a television set hooked up to a fellow traveler's car battery. The astronauts are landing on the moon. The navigator, they say, was Newton.

Looking at my store of facts, I recognize a kind of bell curve. I started with a boundaryless mixture that slowly resolved itself in an increasing store of facts accumulated at home, in school and on through college. But then the facts began to decrease. Evidence remains, evanescent lines recorded on screens. Is my mind just such a screen, recording the evidence of the senses and then projecting realities that correspond exactly to what is on my screen? A friend says he does not understand those people who touch a chair and say "That's not there!" Something is there I think, else I would not have any evidence. But does it look the same to everyone? Is my green or yellow or red the same as yours? Or do we just all have the same evidence and the learned response that what each of us sees is red or yellow or green, so that we stop or slow down or start in unison, and do not crash into each other?

Perhaps it does not matter. I remain convinced that there are on occasions things that are given, that are there and independent of me, and that if I do not pay attention to them, I will be hurt. Yes, Virginia, there really are facts, even if I am not always certain just what they really are. And facts, as much as the faith event, need to be acknowledged. An idea that is contrary to fact will not last very long. People do try, however – I recall the seminary professor ending his lecture of the day with the statement "Thus, you see, our thesis is proven, despite the facts." But ideas that are contrary to fact do not last forever. The facts, like murder, will out!

I take it as a given, therefore, that those things that I see as facts must be respected, acknowledged and accounted for in any thoughts, ideas or systems of knowledge that attempt to be consistent and in development of a faith event. It will not be enough to propose a set of ideas that squares with the faith event, although any system must do at least that much. The system will also have to deal with the facts, neither ignoring nor contradicting them.

Evolution in the broad sense – that there has been a connected development from the start of the universe through molecules and living entities up to human beings – is, for me, a fact. I also take the quantum world – the both/and nature of reality at its core and the strange relationship to the observer that exists there – as a fact. It is true that these "facts" may yet be only solidified theories ultimately recognized as false. They are not yet quite the same quality as the heliocentric nature of our solar system. But they are strong enough that I cannot disregard them. No world of ideas will be satisfactory if it ignores these facts.

4. Faith – the Event Open to Transcendence

When we ask "What does it all mean?" the primary and most important question is the implied one: "Is there any meaning at all?" Faith answers "Yes" to that question. But what is faith? My answer, at least at this part of my journey, is that faith is a unique kind of event in my life. It is not a set of ideas or a creed or an image. It is an immediate experience in which we are grasped at the very core and heart of our being by an encounter with a center or ground that relates to all that is including myself, and which at the same time relates me to all that is. The experience is something of which we are conscious but it is not something that is initially caught in thought. Emptying the mind of ideas is the classic way of making oneself ready for the experience; it cannot be obtained by sitting down and taking thought.

The faith event, as I sense I have experienced it, has both an element of being inside me at the very deepest level of my being, and also of being outside me. My self and others are joined in a way that immediately is felt as right, all encompassing, a completion of existence. It is where we contact what the poet Gerard Manley Hopkins in "God's Grandeur" called "the dearest freshness deep down things" and find it is present everywhere. There is a "given" quality to it that puts it beyond my control, and provides the sense of insight into that which transcends all particulars. Faith is at root an event that is open, and opens us, to transcendence of this fact I call myself and all the other facts in my world of experience.

But there is also a cooperative feel to the event. It is *given* from without, but it is given to *me*, so that the giver, the recipient and the giving are but different sides of a total experience that cannot finally be broken down and analyzed without removing ourselves from the immediacy of the event. The best that we can do with analysis and words and thoughts is as the ancient command to physicians: "First, do no harm."

Once the faith event has occurred it cannot be eradicated or completely forgotten. I can deliberately obscure it or pretend that I have not heard an eternal "Yes," but it lies there in my life for all my days. It may be that we all have it in childhood and that would explain the fundamental optimism that seems to characterize children and all adults who have not hidden their earliest experience under a bundle of theories and ideas. Following the advice of the mystics of all religions can prepare us for its reappearance in our adult lives – take some time out, empty your mind of all its raging ideas, meditate. The event will reassert itself in each of our lives if we are open to it. It may take a long time if you are as stubborn and opinionated as I was. But it will not finally be denied to all who are open to the transcendence of being.

In my life faith has come mostly in bursts of seeing beyond the surface of plants and trees, mountains and oceans. I have had occasional glimpses of the same underlying ground in relations with other persons, and have wished that I was more open to events in which I and thou deepens into the union of both of us in God. That would seem to be a better way, although perhaps it is just a case of thinking the grass greener in my neighbor's garden. Whatever the circumstances in which the faith event occurs in an individual's life, the end result seems the same. I know beyond any expressions of knowing that there is a reality underlying and uniting all that is. If I do not know what that means in terms of the ideas my mind creates, I still know that no such ideas can destroy the reality of the faith event, because it lies behind and under all that I can think or imagine. The faith event determines the validity of my ideas, not the other way around.

5. Theories – the Frameworks for Facts

Theories are complex sets of ideas designed to explain and clarify the facts found in the world in which we live. Start with a set of facts – apples dropping from trees, balls rolling down an incline, a moon circling the earth and the earth itself circling the sun. How can we understand this? Is there some connection between the observed facts? Can we do better than just say "That's the way it is"? Newton came up with his laws of motion as an explanation of certain observations. And it worked. The theory he devised really did explain and clarify what was going on. And, what's more, it allowed him and others to predict how events not yet observed might occur. The predictions were tested by experiments and added proof to the validity of the theory. But it all started out as a complex of ideas designed to scratch our itch for understanding, for finding a pattern in events, for seeking the reasons and causes that moved the world about us.

Typically a theory goes through several stages of development. First it is a kind of brilliant guess, a hypothesis, intended to show the underlying pattern in what may have seemed unrelated observed facts. If it satisfactorily relates all the observations, the hypothesis becomes a full fledged theory, ready for predictions and further observations. If the observations concur with the predictions, the theory moves toward becoming a scientific truth. After some time and many observations, the theory itself may come to be regarded as a fact.

Theories utilize familiar ideas and images to explain facts. The Greeks were familiar with circles and thought the circle the perfect geometric shape. They also knew what crystal was and its quality of transparency. When they sought an explanation of the apparent movement of the sun, moon and stars, they theorized that each of those bodies moved in concentric circles around the earth, their paths etched into crystal spheres surrounding the earth. In modern science we see the same thing at work when Bohr uses the planetary system as a model for electrons in the atom circling the nucleus. It is something we all do, none so naturally as children who have not yet lost spontaneous imagination. Once driving down a street full of puddles after a rainstorm, my younger son saw a film of oil on a pool of water, the swirls of oil iridescent with color. He did not know about the refraction of light or the qualities of oil, but he already knew quite a bit about things broken and he had seen colored arcs in the sky. So he said, "Look, a broken rainbow." If we are fortunate not to have closed our imaginations to new images, all of us can see broken rainbows.

Nobody today knows with certainty whether Archimedes really cried "Eureka" (Greek for "I've found it") when he discovered a method for purifying gold, but he might well have. All good theories have an "Aha!" quality. I have a sudden surge of excitement because a new idea has an immediate feeling of fitting the facts. Even before the experiments confirm the discovery, I have a sense that I have found what I was looking for, that a circle has been completed. If it feels like just one more dumb idea, then it probably is, and I would do better to keep on looking.

But theories, even those most exciting at their discovery, do not last forever. Thomas Kuhn's book *The Structure of Scientific Revolutions* talks about the breakdown of theories. Small clouds, no larger than a person's hand, begin to appear on the horizon. The theory neither predicted them nor seems able to explain them. Those holding the theory scramble to modify the theory, to make additions or deletions here and there. The theory grows more complicated, while the unexplained observations continue to multiply. Finally a new theory is offered, one which can explain all of the observed facts, both the new ones and the ones explained by the previous theory. The game goes on, with new predictions and new observations. A classic case is the efforts of those holding the Ptolemaic (geocentric) theory of the universe to explain, through ever more complicated sets of epicycles the expanding observations of the stars and planets. The increasingly obvious breakdown of that theory made the discovery of a new theory inevitable. If Galileo and Copernicus had never lived, someone would still have discovered that the earth moves. When the student is ready, the teacher appears – it applies to societies and cultures as well as to individuals!

It is one of the great ironies that human beings, so restlessly curious about how things work, should hold on so tenaciously to the theories of the past. Perhaps my willingness to entertain a new theory is inversely proportional to the amount of time and effort I have invested in the old theory. Position and prestige, sometimes even my very idea of who I am seems to hang in the balance. When I do not accept the death of theories that have outlived their usefulness, I am condemned to join the ranks of reactionary naysayers moaning the loss of once beautiful but now dead worlds. There is no one so bitter, so angry and so ready to denounce as the defender of a theory that has seen its day come and go.

6. Beliefs – Theories of Faith

The second aspect of the question "What does it all mean?" is the question "Given that there is a meaning, what is that meaning?" Beliefs are simply theories, but theories developed to provide an explanation of what occurs in faith events. Beliefs differ from theories designed to explain observable facts, because beliefs strive to explain the directly experienced but not objectively observable event of faith. But beliefs and faith are far more often confused or even identified than are theories and facts. The creeds and statements of belief put forth by religious communities as statements of their faith are often taken as that faith itself. Faith is not a belief; it is instead an event that, reflected upon after its occurrence, brings out our curiosity and our desire for explanation, leading to the formation of beliefs. Faith is a shattering event, central to our conviction of meaning. Beliefs are words, ideas, images – the concrete, discrete thoughts our minds form and then use to try the impossible task of getting a hold on our faith. God, one of my professors once said, is an ineffable (unspeakable) mystery. But, he said, since they are human and carry a built in urge to put it all into words, theologians spend their lives trying to "eff the ineffable."

One way of putting this is to say it's all theology – scriptures and creeds as well as systems of thought. I grew up in a tradition that separated belief from theology. Beliefs were founded in the scriptures and expressed in creeds like the Nicene Creed set down in the fourth century. Theology was commentary upon the beliefs. Beliefs were eternally true; theology was theory and opinion that could change. But if faith is a preverbal event and beliefs are the human verbal response to that event, then there is no room for any belief making claim to the unchangeable quality of the event of faith.

Beliefs, if they are to be an explanation, must utilize what is known and familiar in order to explain what underlies all thought and therefore is not fully reducible to any thought. We call the underlying reality we have experienced in a faith event "God" or "Great Spirit" or something else, and then we go further and talk about that reality as a Father or a King or a shepherd or hunter or whatever it is in our daily life that seems to us to have characteristics that "fit" or are "appropriate" to that which we want to explain. And then, if we know what we are doing, we go on to say that of course God or the Great Spirit is not exactly like that, because what we have experienced underlies everything but is not the same as anything in particular. The image or idea we use is only like it in some way not entirely clear. It helps to explain because it is taken from some already existing part of our experience that we are familiar with and think we understand.

The fact that our beliefs use things and ideas familiar in daily experience to point toward and assist in understanding the faith event limits those beliefs to just those things and ideas that are available to us in our particular time and place. Using the idea of a king or a kingdom as a symbol of God and God's territory will be a useful choice for those familiar with kings and kingdoms. It would not be a helpful choice for those whose experience of kings is unlikely to be more than a visit to the street outside Buckingham Palace for the changing of the guard. I *can* come to some understanding of the preferred ideas past ages utilized to develop into words their faith events, and this can be a helpful and rewarding task. But is this the only path, one required of all who would understand? I have to ask why God or anyone else would choose to make things so difficult. You would have to assume that one culture had a lock on perfection – that it had achieved the most that could ever be achieved in the way of ideas, images and systems of understanding. History may not tell us a lot, but surely it tells us that cultures come and go, mostly go. I have spent much time learning the elements of the great medieval synthesis. My faith does not stretch to believing that effort is required of my contemporaries. Like the cartoon child looking at the fancy plate in front of him, I say it's spinach and I say the hell with it.

The holders of mere theories about simple facts can become hardened in their position, determined to demonstrate the falseness of any competing theories. The holders of beliefs can take this opposition to new heights. Witness the long sad history of the persecution by Christians of other Christians who did not share the same beliefs about their common Christian faith. All those wars and inquisitions, condemnations and threats, hatred on the faces, hatred in the hearts. Can this be what Jesus meant by the law of love?

An argument over a phrase in a statement of belief split the Christian Church in the early part of its second millennium. The argument was over the abstruse issue – a distant outpost in the dominion of a vast theological empire – whether the Spirit, the third person of the Trinity, proceeded or emanated from both the second (the Son) and first (the Father) persons of the Trinity, or from the Father alone. The Eastern (Orthodox) Church said

Father alone, the Western (Roman) Church said Father
and Son ("filioque"), and division took place. People can
still take it seriously. During my time at a seminary north
of New York City, a car was sent to Peekskill to pick up
one of the more colorful faculty members returning from
the city. He asked the driver to make a detour and had
the car stopped when it was in front of the local Orthodox
church. Rolling down the window, sticking his head out
and shaking his fist, he yelled "Filioque, you bastards!"
Doubtless an improvement over a previous age when his
spirit might have compelled him to burn the heretics.

7. But Remember – It Moves!

I've talked about facts, faith, theories and beliefs as
if they were all clearly distinguishable from each other.
They are not the same as each other, but it would be a
mistake to think that distinction of definition means there
is no overlap. My left brain logical way of analysis leads
me in this direction – part of me (the part that builds
systems of ideas!) thinks that reality is made up of discrete
atoms and that, if I carefully chop that world up, I will
come to an irreducible number of clear and distinct concepts representing entities completely clear and distinct
in themselves. My right brain (which is the part of me
that seems open to faith events). however, murmurs that
it's just not that way. Everything real does interlap and
connect. My right and left brains are somehow connected.
Facts demand theories of explanation and theories in turn
become facts, perhaps to be overturned with the passage
of time and place into new facts and theories. Theories
and facts can lead us to faith events and faith events can
move compellingly into beliefs.

One day many years ago I was reading an eminent
theologian's arguments for his theory on something or
other. When he came to "Twenty-seventhly . . ." with many
pages yet to come, I quit. We people of the West are like
weight lifters who have worked only on one arm. That

arm is hugely muscled, while the other one is thin and weak. We like to turn to our left brain and let it do all the work. It is good and necessary not to get too hung up in definitions and logical connections and extensions of ideas. Something requiring 27 reasons (and more to come!) for its proof may be valid but it surely can't be very interesting! It is also good to keep in mind Emerson's statement: "A foolish consistency is the hobgoblin of little minds, adored by . . . philosophers and divines" (*Self-Reliance*).

8. Truth and Validity

Suppose that I am looking at a mountain on whose right side I see a large pointed rock jutting outward into space, crowned with a tall pine tree. And suppose I am talking to you on the telephone and telling you about the mountain. You tell me I've got it all wrong. The rock and the pine tree are on the left side of the mountain. We argue, look again, check our definitions of right and left. And then one of us gets a bright idea. Perhaps we are not both standing on the same side of the mountain. Perhaps we are standing on opposite sides of the mountain. Neither of our statements is absolutely true. Each of them is valid in relation to where we each stand.

What can be said about the *truth* of a *belief*? At the risk of becoming enmeshed in just one more argument, my answer is that very little can be said about the truth (or falsity) of beliefs. Let me explain. I think the term *truth* is best used to express a quality of events and facts (at least of those facts that are not just conclusions based on misunderstood appearances). Truth, used this way, expresses a characteristic of all being, a term pointing to the fact that this being is just what it is and nothing else. My faith event is true – it was really there, it really happened, and nothing can ever make that event a nonevent.

To the extent that theories or beliefs adequately state the truth of faith or facts, it is possible to say that the theories and beliefs are "true." Possible, but not, I think, helpful. Theories can change in the light of new facts or fuller understandings of existing facts. Beliefs too can change as a new framework of familiar circumstances leads us to speak in new ways of the faith event.

It creates less confusion if we adopt the habit of thinking of our theories and beliefs as valid rather than true. They are valid – have a real value – to the extent they reflect the truth of the faith event or facts they seek to explain. To the extent that a belief falls short of full explanation (and the very nature of a faith event, underlying and going beyond any explanation makes it certain that all beliefs fall short of the reality it tries to grasp) beliefs are invalid. Further, to the extent beliefs use ideas or images unfamiliar to the believer, they are also invalid. They are not *true*, either in the sense that they either fully express the underlying reality or in the sense that their validity extends to all times and places.

It follows that a belief can be valid for one time and place but not for another. It can become invalid as it fails to enlighten the believers about the nature of their faith, which alone is true. If we were living in the fourth or fifth century, with a good education in Greek philosophy, we might find it very useful – highly valid – to explain God as three persons (*prosopa*) while only one in nature (*phusis*), and to understand Jesus as having two natures while being one person. If, in the 20th century the Greek understanding of person and nature is literally all Greek to us, then such a statement of belief becomes invalid – not in any sense that it is false but simply in the sense that it no longer serves the function for which it was designed. It no longer has the capacity to explain *to us* that faith event which alone has the quality of truth.

One belief can be more valid than another belief. Each person working out of a faith event finds a belief system that is valid in relation to that person's faith. But belief systems are not purely private. They arise out of familiar daily experiences and so can be assessed to a large extent within the experiences of others. We can enter into a common effort and profitably discuss with our contemporaries which elements out of our familiar experiences might provide the best system of beliefs for our time and place

I don't believe that God talks only to me or even only to the people in my cultural neighborhood. God is either present to everyone or present to no one. If we can keep in mind that beliefs are human efforts to comprehend what is finally incomprehensible, then we might be moved to listen to each other with greater respect and greater patience. Even beliefs that would be invalid for us can tell us something about the world of another believer and may in that way give us insights that our own limited experience would have missed. The best reason for not climbing into a hole with my own version of belief is that when I do I am keeping myself from hearing what others hear, seeing what they see.

A Working Hypothesis

When dealing with quantum reality one of the most exciting aspects of the work is that you can't ever be entirely certain of what is going to happen next. Predictability and control are lost, only to be replaced by excitement and sudden openings to new vistas. We are learning that all life partakes of this unpredictability and excitement, and that the biggest mistake we have made in the past is to think that we can, given enough thought, know it all, control it all and make life utterly predictable. We have talked about "fine tuning" so that life moves forward in perfect harmony, all things just the way we think we want them. Maybe we are at last learning that is not the way reality operates. You can fine tune radios, but you can't adjust reality.

So I don't want to make the mistake of setting up a program for the rest of this book that will assure specific conclusions. It has to be a work in progress, which will unfold in the course of the writing, taking unexpected new paths and leading to possibilities and actualities not foreseen at the start.

Having said all that, I confess to a working hypothesis, an initial structure within which I begin. It may be narrowed or, more likely, exploded beyond its initial boundaries as the work develops. But at the beginning, I operate under the hypothesis that my tradition of Roman Catholicism (and Christianity in general) has a bare bones, stripped down as much as possible without passing beyond the world of words, belief in a reality called God, a revelation of that reality in a historical person called Jesus, and a community of those sharing a faith event expressing itself in beliefs about God, Jesus, themselves and the world.

The second and central aspect of the working hypothesis is that the Christian faith event has been expressed in beliefs that use ideas, language and images important to the faithful at the time of their original expression. The faith event does not change, but the belief systems must change as the community of the faithful passes into different times and places with different familiar ideas and images and a different language of expression.

Instead of getting tangled in the ways this change has or could have taken place, it may be useful to ask a question. If Jesus were to be born today, what would he have to say about himself and the world in which he found himself? Would he even come again as a man, or would the agent of God's revelation be a woman this time? How would he or she express his or her ideas and, more importantly, how would we, today's listeners, express our response? I do not think that we would formulate our beliefs in the way valid for the first century community or that of the middle ages or even the 19th century.

Expressions of belief have a life cycle – birth, growth and decay. Underlying my working hypothesis is a sense that we live in a time when the traditional system, a mixture of ideas and images formed over nearly 2,000 years, has decayed to the point where it is no longer capable of helping us understand the meaning of our lives and of existence itself. John XXIII, the Pope who called the Second Vatican Council, must have caught the same whiff of dry rot when he threw open a window in the Vatican and called for fresh air. It is time to work on the formulation of a new set of beliefs, a new way of talking about the Christian faith event that both preserves that event and brings everything else into our lives into a framework of relationships corresponding, for us and our time, to that underlying unity faith asserts.

Think of it as changing modes of transportation. We are still trying to get to the Garden of Eden, but we're traveling in an airplane instead of on foot or by horse and carriage. And keep in mind that it's not the final mode. Spaceships and rides through intergalactic wormholes and other possibilities that we don't yet know how to build or haven't even thought of will come along to replace our efforts. But we progress by working at it, not just standing here.

A World of Whuffs

A salesman came to my office one day. For some reason we started talking about our children and the wonderful curiosity they often showed. He told me about one of his who had this curiosity to a much greater extent than usual. Every day was full of questions beginning "What if . . . ?" Only the child was too young to pronounce all the words clearly, and it kept coming out "Whuff." So the family started calling ideas about how things might be if thought of in a different way "Whuffs."

This is a book of "Whuffs." I propose to take certain aspects of the faith event and certain facts and lay a "Whuff" on them. Each of the next five chapters will take up a central issue or complex of related issues found in the expression of Christian faith and inquire whether it might be stated in a way that brings to bear our own experience in this present space and time.

What if we thought about God or Jesus or the church or the fall in terms of evolution and quantum reality rather than the way we learned in our youth?

What if we dared to eat a peach?

CHAPTER THREE

The Now and Future God

I greet him the days I meet him, and bless when I understand.

> – Gerard Manley Hopkins,
> "The Wreck of the Deutschland"

If there were no internal propensity to unite, even at a prodigiously rudimentary level – indeed in the molecule itself – it would be physically impossible for love to appear higher up.

> – Pierre Teilhard de Chardin, *The Phenomenon of Man*

Even bein' Gawd ain't a bed of roses.

> – Marcus Cook Connelly, *The Green Pastures*

On the one side. Total darkness. No sound. Emptiness. A void, yet not absolutely nothing. The emptiness has a reality. It does not yet exist, nothing outside itself. Just pure potential. The ultimate possibility of all that might be or never be. No ears to hear, no hairs to feel a breeze. If there had been, a dynamo ready to turn might have been sensed.

On the other side. A gigantic burst of energy mushrooms opposite the pregnant void, a cataclysm of sound and fury and light. More sparks than can return to the void before more surface. Now an eddy here, a current there and particles collide and merge, swirling and surging. Atoms are formed and out of them molecules.

Ages pass. Still no ears, no eyes, but now water and air, earth and fire. And self-recreating cells, then multicellular organisms. Emerging from the water like the primordial sparks, they breathe and grow.

A spark finally shines late in the cosmic day. It has a reflecting shell and sees itself as well as the things around it. It smiles. Then the void folds inward, also smiles, and is finally able to say: "It is good."

In the Beginning

My wife Kathleen, our three children and I came to Texas in 1980. I was fresh out of Vanderbilt Law School. Nashville in the late '70s was still an old Southern city. I had briefly thought of staying there to practice law but the thought faded as I realized that my grandchildren might be taken as natives but I would always be a damn Yankee. Weary of being asked who my daddy was and where my family came from, I struck out for Texas, having been assured by the son of a senior partner in the law firm hiring me that "nobody down here is more than second generation and most aren't even that."

On my arrival in Corpus Christi the Young Lawyers Association promptly invited me to join. My wife just as promptly pointed out that I, then 45 years old, might be a *new* lawyer but I could hardly qualify as a *young* lawyer. I didn't join, but I did plunge into the legal community and the practice of law with a mixture of fear and excitement.

The dress-for-success in Nashville advice (manufactured by the law students) was that white shoes, polyester suits, preferably brown, green or burgundy, and gravy spots on the tie were proper. I had been inclined to think that Texas lawyers would come to court in Levis and string ties, if ties at all. I soon learned that the bankers and the lawyers (all the folk on the elevator early in the morning) had a deep desire to be more Eastern than any Ivy Leaguer. Navy blue and charcoal gray, with or without pinstripe, white shirts and small patterned ties were the uniform of choice.

Somebody finally told me that the people wearing Levis and Rolex watches were the oil and ranching crowd – the ones with all the money (it was still early in the '80s, well before the big bust). I'm still not rich but I have finally succeeded in mostly staying away from places that want suits. My remaining ties are much narrower than they should be, but I'm confident they will be worn so little they will still have life when fashion declares once again that narrow is the style of choice.

When I started practicing law I did a substantial amount of real estate work. In law school, the course on real property had illustrated how quirky that area of the law was, no doubt as befitted something so important to most people. In Texas the law was newer than the old laws of the eastern United States, which often reflected English common law of the 17th century or earlier. But Texas has been, at one time or another, under six different flags and its real property laws, although newer, had their own complexities.

Particularly important and the source of many disputes was the issue of good title. The "chain" of title was critical, each owner tracing its right to the immediately preceding owner, back and back. In Texas, you didn't have to go far back in the chain of owners to find grants from Spanish kings. Whether all the lands had been properly transferred during the change from Spanish and French to Mexican and on to Texan sovereignty and finally to the laws of the United States and the State of Texas (with a short interval for the Confederacy), to say nothing of a healthy dose of frontier ways, was not always as clear as a cautious lawyer might wish.

So I laughed (and learned to deal with a less than perfect world) when I read about the Louisiana lawyer who represented a seller and was much harassed by the buyer's attorney over the question of good title. After lengthy and subtle exchanges, he wrote a letter to his adversary, detailing the various deeds, all properly made, executed and filed of record, going back to owners in the early 19th century who, as the lawyer wrote, "received their title by grant from the Congress of the United States of America, which had purchased Louisiana and environs from the Empire of France as authorized by Napoleon Bonaparte, its emperor. Napoleon Bonaparte had been anointed by the Pope, who was the Vicar of Jesus Christ, the Son of God. *God created the world, including but not limited to that part of Louisiana in which the described real estate is situated.* I hope this puts to rest your questions about my client's good title to the property."

It's Why, Not How

Stories of creation by God or the gods are commonly found among the world's religions. The idea of God as creator is not peculiar to Western Judaeo-Christian religion, although its particular formulation in the Old Testament Book of Genesis is. The common thread is that there is some force, power, being or beings that has brought into existence everything we see about us in the physical world and in fact everything that exists other than the creating force.

In that limited sense, the idea of God as creator is completely consistent and in accord with all that I have experienced as the core of faith and the underlying ground of belief. That which came upon me in my garden and with which I felt a unity was also that which spoke of power and relationship to all that was, is and would be – source, foundation and, in Paul Tillich's term, the *ground* of being. So far, all systems are Go.

Genesis is a wonderful and fascinating book, and its story of creation majestic and memorable. Somehow, however, that story with its emphasis on God as the creator-source of all that is, has become tarnished and grown somewhat dim from squabbles and discussions that focus on pieces of the story, obscuring the central theme. Evolution with its picture of gradual change over vast periods of time has been bombarded by proponents of Biblical inerrancy. God created the world in six days and on the seventh rested – six real and countable days. If I go outside during the day and watch the change from morning to evening, I understand how easy it was to claim that the sun moves around the earth. If I, a being whose life span is measured in decades rather than light years, look at the world as a whole, with all its freshness and beauty, and the obvious stability of all things in it, it is equally understandable that the world be thought of as young, pulled just as it is into being, a beautiful Venus rising from the shell of God.

Then there are all the medieval theologians, their progeny still repeating the words "creation out of nothing." Eager to emphasize that there was nothing existing prior to divine creation, no unformed matter and nothing like paint-by-number sheets awaiting only the addition of some heavenly oils, the theologians looked at the process of creation, insisting at every opportunity that God had nothing to work with other than the divine creativity itself. It's not wrong and perhaps not even invalid; the problem is one of misplaced emphasis.

But these emphases and squabbles have to do with the *how* of creation, not with the much more interesting and fundamental question about the *why* of creation. I was reminded of this a few days ago when I came across a cartoon picturing a cow sitting in the witness chair of a courtroom. The lawyer questioning the cow is saying: "Look. We know *how* you did it – *how* is no longer the question. What we now want to know is *why*. . . . Why now, brown cow?"

The standard Christian answers are that God created the world in order that the divine glory be manifest, and that God created human persons in particular in order that they might love and obey and be happy with God forever in heaven. I confess I never found these answers very satisfying or enlightening. They seemed, I felt, to raise more questions than they answered. Why would God want or care to manifest divine glory? Was God some kind of eternal yuppie who needed the assurance of brand names and glitz to feel valuable and secure? Was God the original Sun King needing a Fontainebleu to reflect his brightness?

And what about us? It sounded pretty good at first glance, but on sober reflection it looked like more of the glory idea. I kept wondering what value we might possibly have. A relationship where everything came from one side and nothing from the other didn't sound like a happy one. Why all the pain and suffering if the aim was to be happy forever? Was there perhaps something more fundamental going on in creation than what appeared to be only the satisfaction of a divine whim?

Creation and Self-Knowledge

Plato taught us that for all types of things there is one perfect form or Idea. There is an Idea of human, of rose, of horse, of what you will. The Ideas are perfect and unchangeable. Individual roses and horses and humans are all changeable and different from each other, but all humans and all horses and all roses are also essentially alike because they participate in the Idea of human or horse or rose. Christian thinkers lit upon this theory like bees drawn to pollen and believed that they had found the perfect location for Plato's Ideas: the mind of the Biblical God. And so, in the popular view, God reviewed the divine Ideas and decided to create some particular objects, moon and stars and sun and animals and plants and the rest, based on the Ideas in the divine mind. The idea of creative action still has the popular denotation of

being an activity that brings into existence some preconceived and pre-existing idea lodged in the mind of the
creator. How many of us never see our own creativity
because we think we don't have the required clear and
distinct ideas?

There is, however, another way to understand the
creative process. It is not a technical process of making
something that illustrates a clear idea in the creator's
mind. Instead it is a process that makes something outside
of and distinct from the creator which, simultaneous with
its existence as different and other than the creator, reveals to the creator who and what the creator is. The
creative act is primary, ideas are secondary.

I think of working on this book. It started with an
urge to put down what might seem satisfying as an explanation of my experiences. But there was no clear idea of
what that explanation might be when I started. "How do
I know what I think until I hear what I have to say?" ran
through my mind as work progressed. Dead ends, sudden
turns, surprise vistas, hills and valleys unrolled as I struck
the computer keys. Ideas raced ahead and then went
backwards. The experience was one of learning as I moved
along. It was certainly not a dictation, just a constant effort
to put something into words that connected, felt right in
light of something that was there within but not explicit.
Prior to putting pages on paper, this book existed only
as a potential object. It needed the act of ongoing creation
to bring it into actual existence.

Anything and everything can be helpful when the
creative force is at work. The glint of sunlight from the
pool could turn to a thought of creation reflecting God.
A chance line in a book I had started to read for no
particular reason could suddenly open up a new movement in a chapter. I sensed relief and joy when the appropriate words came, frustration when they did not.
Inside the block of stone was something struggling to get
out. When the chisel hit flesh, the flesh knew it and cried
out with relief at being freed.

I think of the birth and growth of my children, Sean, Colin and Megan. Each one is different from the others and from me and Kathleen. Yet there are similarities and hidden relations to us and generations past. Two weeks ago I visited my great aunt. She tells me that Colin looks like my uncle Bob, who died before I was born. I never much liked the game of pointing to a nose and saying that came from a grandfather, or a chin came from a distant aunt or uncle. I thought I was just me, nobody else. And I suppose my children feel the same. But there is a relationship through the generations and it has to be acknowledged. At the same time there is something new, never before seen. Both their old and their new facets give me a reflected glimpse of who I am and who I am not.

I do not know for sure what I have had to do with all this accumulation that now walks abroad as Sean, Colin and Megan. Yet I learn from each of them something about myself. Some things are painful, walking wounds that I have caused and in which I recognize my own wounds. Someone said we are all adult children of adult children. But we see our childhood in a different and often healing light when we see it in the acts of others.

And there are good things, too. I do not think I did it all wrong, although there is much I would change if a second chance could come. But there is a good deal of healthy independence and a strong desire to search. When they were small, they liked to climb the trees in our front yard. Despite our fears of falling, we let them go, often to the very top, where they swayed in the wind, level with the roof on our two-story house. A neighbor called in outrage, demanding if I knew "what my children were doing?" I did and took the chance she would not report child abuse. But they did not fall (except Colin at Boy Scout camp, where he fractured both wrists when jumping from a mound to a tree). They did, I think, experience some sense of self reliance and the thrill of exploring. I think it was worth the risks; I hope they do too. Their adventurous spirit suggests to me that I might have some of the same spirit, however hidden or repressed. Maybe there are still trees left for me to climb.

It is never quite clear what I had to do with my children's bodies, character, successes and failures. But in some way it is all enlightening. I learn more about myself as they move through life. Besides all the fun and pain of watching them grow, there is that invaluable even if often obscured self knowledge.

Looking back over my nearly 60 years, it seems to me that my whole life has been something of a creation. Things often happened by a sudden chance. I decided to go to law school when I was 42 after reading a headline in the *Wall Street Journal* about the need for more lawyers. I might not have done it if the headline had not appeared at the right time. But it was not entirely a random event. It fit with occasional thoughts of studying law and reappearing wishes that I had done that earlier in life. Most of the decisions over the years have been small ones, but they have added up to something that I call myself, and that I now see I was making day in and year out. I know who I am, although not entirely, by what I have done and am doing as well as what I hear myself saying. I will know a little more tomorrow.

In late August of 1994, I drove Megan back to Georgetown University for her sophomore year. The trunk was loaded with Colin's belongings, later to be delivered at the University of Notre Dame. The back seat was full of Megan's clothes. The trip, I told myself, was at least in part to prove that I was still up to a long road journey. Even more so it was a time to reclaim a part of the past.

Driving through Pennsylvania, I visited and took pictures of seven different houses, ones where I had lived with my parents and then the houses where my paternal great grandmother had lived and where my maternal grandmother had taken me in on so many visits and vacations. Memories of the small child I once was flooded in at all of them, but none more so than when I saw my great-grandmother's house, now beige instead of white, the picket fence gone, a two-car garage in the back yard where once I had played among the flowering iris. Suddenly it was the spring of 1939.

I was always tall and thin, but at four-and-a-half the purple and yellow iris were not much below eye level. They moved slowly in the late afternoon breeze, casting shadows on the white shed wall standing guard at the bottom of my great grandmother's back yard. The flat leaves were spears and swords and I ravaged the stalks for a handful, each one's light green staining darker as I squeezed it and stabbed at black knights and dragons roaming the yard. Spent sword leaves soon littered the grass and the brown earth bordering the flower beds.

 Weary from battle, I climbed into the yard swing, a truncated A-frame wooden contraption with connected seats facing each other. By pulling on the side supports I was able to get the seats moving slightly. With some further squirming of my body back and forth, the swing took on a respectable but creaking motion, and I rested in the warmth of the afternoon sun. I turned and looked at the house. Like the shed, the swing and the picket fence that surrounded the yard, it was white. Narrow shadows between the horizontal strips of wood siding stood out straight as lines on a sheet of ruled paper.

 The house rose up from the side of a hill. On my left a retaining wall held the yard from collapsing into the house next door. The roofs of the neighbor's house and those beyond it fell down the hill like rickety steps towards the town below. I had been down there with my parents earlier in the afternoon. The stores in the small Pennsylvania mining town were closed and the streets almost deserted. Uncle Ambrose and Aunt Ann ran O'Connor's Bar & Grill, a coal miner's bar. I'd heard my father call it the "bucket of blood" and sensed that the family did not entirely approve running a bar, or at least one like this. The bar was closed, but we were let in by a side door which opened into a stairway to the apartment above. I could smell stale beer everywhere.

Once we had visited on a Saturday and had gone into the bar to see Uncle Ambrose. It was dark and cool and filled with a low rumble of voices. Ambrose, dark eyed and white haired, stood behind the bar with a towel, wiping glasses. I was frightened by the sudden silence of the customers, some of whom were staring at me, and glad when we went upstairs to the apartment.

Outside the picket fence to my right was a sidewalk and a strip of land angling up to the street. Across the street was Aunt Laura's house. It was white, too, but larger and higher than great grandmother's, with a porch that stretched from the front around the side and a bay window. Laura's husband, Charlie, owned the local drugstore and was usually at work. He was there today, too, even though it was Sunday. Aunt Pauline said the priest was angry with Charlie because he kept the drugstore open on Sunday morning and people went there instead of to Sunday Mass. She said the priest was going to denounce my uncle from the altar. She didn't seem to think very much of the priest, but I sensed she was not pleased with what she called the disgrace.

Aunt Laura had three sons. They were in college. Once, when I visited my great grandmother last Christmas, they had been home and had set up model trains in Aunt Laura's living room. The memory of the trains moving around the tree and out over the carpet, circling the chairs and tables, came back to me now. I desperately wanted a model train. No one I knew except Aunt Laura's sons and my friend Bobby had even one, let alone several. Bobby's was made in Germany and was a passenger train, with lights in the cars that shone through the windows as the train ceaselessly circled on its track.

Inside the house, my great grandmother, Aunt Pauline and my parents were talking in the sitting room. I had spent some time there when we first arrived. The sitting room had a gray carpet with a blue border along which ran thin curlicues of light tan, like the tendrils on the grape vines in the back yard arbor. I liked to follow each tendril, pursuing it from its solitary start near the middle of the carpet border into ever expanding swirls as it made its way towards the corner of the carpet, pretending it was a path towards a secret castle or the lair of a monster. Only if I kept squarely on the center of the tendril, refusing to turn aside onto any of the false trails, could I hope to reach the treasure.

The sitting room was less formal than the front parlor, which had furniture that was very dark and uncomfortable. Once there had been a funeral, I didn't know whose, and the body had lain in a casket at the end of the parlor, surrounded by bouquets of orange and yellow and white gladioli. I was hurried out of the room as soon as I came in, so I hadn't actually seen the body. I hadn't thought it would frighten me, especially since it was nobody I knew, but now the memories of that incident kept me from paying any more than a brief visit to the room. Still, I went in on almost every visit, because there were three ivory elephants, each larger than the one behind it, marching across an end table. The ivory was yellow and crazed with thin dark lines, as if the elephants had been on their journey for many years. I felt something foreign and strange about them and liked to stand silently and watch their unmoving progress.

The sitting room sofa on which my great grandmother sat was upholstered in shades of brown, its soft material shaved in places so that a pattern of leaves emerged from a darker background. Two upholstered easy chairs, several end tables and floor lamps and a mahogany secretary with glass doors shielding books inside its upper half filled the rest of the room. Thin lace curtains covered the two windows, one looking towards Aunt Laura's house and the other opening onto the sun porch at the front of the house. My favorite thing in the room was a picture of a woman looking from a terrace onto a moonlit lake, a large tree on the right with its leaves arching over the terrace and an urn on the left. The picture both attracted and slightly frightened me, its dark stillness suggesting some menace just beyond the frame.

Great grandmother was very old, her mouth sunken so that her thin jaw appeared to jut out. She had white, thinning hair, and always, when she was downstairs, wore a black dress that reached down to her ankles, with long sleeves and lace around the throat. She was rarely downstairs when I visited. Most of the time she stayed in her bed in the large rear bedroom upstairs. I liked it best when she was downstairs because, on pretext of going to the bathroom, I could go into her room to see the miniature altar set on her dressing table. Centered behind a tray containing a bone handled mirror, comb, brush and other instruments whose use I could not guess, the altar looked like the large marble one in the church I and my parents went to every Sunday. It even had six candles in candlesticks, three on each side of the central tabernacle, the same as those used at High Mass, except that these had tiny electric lights at the top. The lights were always on.

I had heard my father and mother talk about great grandmother. She had gone to bed in 1932 with some illness and Aunt Pauline, a nurse, had come back from Florida to take care of her. I sensed that my parents and the other relatives had difficulty in dealing with great grandmother and did not like her. I liked her because she had given me two dollars at Christmas, placed inside a white envelope with red and green trim and an oval in the center so you knew right away that it held money. She had acknowledged my kiss when they arrived with a barely perceptible nod of her head.

My great grandmother, as well as my parents, Ann and Ambrose, Pauline, Charlie and Laura, and most of the people they knew or talked about over 50 years ago are dead now. I remain, and they remain in my memory, helping to shape but not controlling my present and my future. That child, recognizably myself, has become the person that now sits here in front of a computer, recalling a life and trying to make sense both of it and the wider world. I still like iris and white houses on hills, still like to walk through other people's houses learning who they are from how they surround themselves. But so many changes, so many decisions, so many different ways in which I am now myself. It is all a great adventure whose trail leads from the present back to the earliest moments of consciousness and will continue to move forward until death brings a closure to memory and creation. Outside forces have always acted upon that growing person, and yet I, that person, have been actively involved in the process, consciously or unconsciously pushing forward the frontiers of what I call myself.

The creative movement of a life involves both stability and change. The "I" endures through all of the changes, yet each change subtly shapes and changes that "I." Everything is different and continually new, yet the experience of all that everything remains somehow the same. "In my beginning is my end" (T. S. Eliot, "East Coker").

All that we do has a creative element, whether it is parenting or writing or making a career or something else. And from it we learn who we are. We reduce our potentiality to act. The golden unformed child becomes a man or a woman whose life is created by all the acts and decisions of the child as it grows, as well as all that is done to it. Writers speak of the inner child existing inside each adult. It is in part a creature of fears instilled as it grew. But it is also the remainder of our possibility, waiting to grow into adulthood.

We have no choice in the matter. If we live at all, we are creative. Sometimes the result is bad, sometimes it is good, but the process starts at birth and continues until death. We create or we die. And in the process we learn who we are.

The Image of God

Genesis says that God created us in the divine image. I don't think that means God looks like a man or a woman. I do think that is a way of saying that our creativity is like God's creativity. More, I think it is a way of saying that God must be creative if God is to be God.

"My dad can beat up your dad!" And my God is more perfect than your God! I understand the temptation to think of God as having it all from the very beginning, even before the beginning. When we are young we think our parents are perfect, know everything, are able to do everything. It is understandable and yet it is a vision of youth, not of those who have grown older in this century of change under the harsh light of deconstruction. For better or worse, we look to the future for a golden age, not to the past.

In our time they say the one with the most toys at death wins. It was not so long ago, however, that the reverse was true. The winners were the ones born with the toys. Born poor, you stayed poor; born rich and powerful, you stayed that way. Find somebody who did not fit the strata into which they were born and you knew you were dealing with a changeling – somebody switched at birth from the royal bedroom to the shepherd's cottage. Like oil released at the bottom of a bucket full of water, they would rise to the top. Everybody had his or her "place." And God had the best place of all, at the pinnacle of an ordered, stratified society laid down once and forever, just as it was now and would always be.

For those like myself accustomed to that way of thinking about God, the mind is wrenched by looking at God as creating in order to be more fully God. It implies that God, like us, is incomplete without the act of continuing creation. Yet how can God be incomplete?

God like God's human creatures is incomplete in the sense that God moves from possibility to actuality. We have only a limited amount of possibility. God is limitless possibility, the potentiality that brings everything that is into actual existence, relates to all that was, is and can ever be. We, and all that surrounds us, are manifestations of the possibilities of God. We are incomplete, cannot even exist, without the actualizing power of God. God is incomplete without creation, the eternal process of moving the divine possibilities into existence. And God, like God's creatures, learns the identity of God from the process.

The Evolving God

You can doubtless guess what is coming next. I started this book with concerns about evolution and how traditional ideas of God could fit with an evolving world. God was static, changeless; the world evolving, in flux. I once supposed that this might be the truth of the matter, although it didn't look or feel like anything close to the mark. The ideas appeared to conflict. At any rate, to someone like myself who had a deep intuition that all of reality ought to hang together, it just wasn't very satisfying. Trying to put a square peg into a round hole was, finally, not even interesting.

When I thought of creation as a process whereby I was developing and changing without losing self identity, and learning who I was as I went through the process, God as the creator *par excellence* suddenly made a lot more sense. If God was only God in the process of creation and was eternally learning what it was to be God as the unlimited divine possibilities were reduced to actual existence outside of God, then an evolving world was exactly the kind of world such a God would create. Both God and God's creation were simultaneously evolving!

The old conundrum of God's omniscience versus human free will (if God already knows what we will do, how can it be a free act?) or the debate whether God could be both all powerful and all good (if God is all good, God would prevent evil; if God doesn't prevent evil, then God must either be less than omnipotent or not all good) should have tipped us off that something was a bit awry with the old view of God. Like the Ptolemaic astronomers who kept adding epicycles to epicycles, the medieval theologians and their progeny tried to make sense of these paradoxical problems. The "solution" often seemed to me a cosmic shell game.

The final response was always the same: we just don't understand the ways of God. Well, of course we don't, but that isn't a license to engage in nonsense. It reminded me of one of my philosophy professors who thought he had shown animals didn't have souls – they were unable, he said to talk intelligently. Since all of my dogs have understood what I said to them, despite my ignorance of what they might be saying in response, I had a hard time with the proof that we humans lived on a higher plane than the animals.

God knows all that has existed or exists now. And I don't doubt that God knows all that can be known by a strict deterministic operation of existing forces. But I don't think God knows what the future will bring through the exercise of human free will. Nor is God likely to know the results of that delicate and mysterious movement that sometimes permits the tiniest of physical changes to end in cataclysmic effects, the subtle balance that keeps everything just at the edge but not over the brink of chaos. Like all of us who are involved in the process of evolution, God sits on the edge of the divine throne waiting to see just what will happen next. Nothing more boring than knowing the end of the story!

When I was writing my dissertation at the University of Chicago I spent an evening with one of the faculty hesitantly expressing some of these ideas about an evolving God who actually learned something about the divine self from the process of creating. He reacted violently, not on philosophical or theological grounds so much as on his reading of a certain passage in Scripture. God, he said, didn't learn that he was the Father, God always knew that He was the Father, and if I didn't believe that, then I should go and read the story of the prodigal son in the New Testament. I'd heard the word "father" before I became one, but I didn't know what it really meant until my children were born. I doubt the prodigal son's father did either. And I think God found out what it meant to really be a father when God's creatures started having children. Things come before ideas, Plato notwithstanding.

There may be a hint of all this in Genesis. What did the first person to put the story of creation into words think when he or she put down the words "And God saw that . . . was good." In each case God saw it was good only after the act of creation, not before. Was this an intuition on the part of the human writer that God, like us, must wait until after creation to learn what has been done? I like to think so.

As unlimited possibility, God never changes. As the ongoing creator, reducing possibility to actuality, God is continually self-actualizing, evolving as the ongoing creation unfolds.

Both/And, Not Either/Or

What I am really talking about here is that both the universe and God are relational. Traditional Christianity has focused on the world as something apart from, even opposed to God, and upon God as that sole, preeminent being who is totally other and apart from the world.

What if, as I suspect, this is the wrong way to go about it? Conceived of as inherently apart, the two can never be brought together. There is no way we can move from A (God) to B (the world), because God is so totally other that God could have no need for a world. That there is no good way to move from the world to God, conceived of as initially separate, is demonstrated by the great variety of debate on the traditional ways of proving God's existence from the fact of an existing world. All that midnight oil and intense intellectual maneuvering has proved is that there is no completely satisfactory proof!

The equation is not, "If B, then A." There is no equation – equations are the way our left brain operates and this is not an area where the left brain can produce. The reality is "AB." So, I am saying, then, that if you look carefully at B, the world, you will find A, God, in its midst, at its center, functioning as its ground. If you don't find

A there and experience A as the heart of the reality B, then you will never be able to prove it, no matter how complex and erudite your chain of reasoning.

God and world are not separate realities. God and the world are together a relationship that constitutes the whole of reality. They are like mother and child, husband and wife. No mother without a child, no husband without a wife.

All of this does nothing to answer questions about the how and the when of creation. I leave that to the physicists. Perhaps there was a "big bang," perhaps not. Perhaps there are an infinity of worlds, each one expanding and then collapsing back into the formation of another one, or perhaps even existing separately and contemporaneously. All I want to push here is that the question about the existence of God and God's relation to all else that exists cannot be answered by logical argument. God is discerned, if at all, in the discernment that constitutes our experience of reality. We are what God is and God is what we are because of the essential relationship that constitutes both God and the world.

Purpose But Not Design

In the 18th century the popular argument for the existence of God was William Paley's argument from design. Consider, he said, finding a watch. You would surely conclude that the watch must have had a maker, because its intricate design precluded it happening from chance. In the same way, Paley thought, you would conclude that there must be a cosmic watchmaker. The intricate design of the things we found about us argued for nothing less than design and, therefore, a designer.

Today there is widespread agreement in the scientific community that there is no design. Instead the complexity of all that we perceive about us has developed incrementally over vast periods of time. Chance mutations with those best adapted to the environment preserved by natural selection is the preferred way of explaining the existing complexity. The refutation holding that a monkey pecking at a typewriter would never write *Hamlet* misses the point. The monkey would not write *Hamlet* in a single shot. But, supposing a vast amount of time and a propensity for retaining those letters that coincided with the text of *Hamlet* as they by chance appeared, the monkey might indeed peck out the full play.

Nonetheless, it goes against the grain to think of the world as essentially accidental. And, simply from the purely scientific point of view, the question must arise why or how the environment is structured in just such a way as to encourage a development in complexity leading to consciousness and self-consciousness. That everything is an accident is not a very interesting idea!

In keeping with the increasing evidence from the study of quantum phenomena, some contemporary scientists have proposed that there is an anthropic principle at work – for the world to be a world, observation is required, and observation presupposes a conscious observer. Design is not what is at work; there is no already conscious creator making a world in the image of the creator's ideas. But there is an inner urging, a push or a drive towards consciousness and even on to self-consciousness.

It does not seem to me accidental that this idea of an anthropic principle at work in the evolution of the world fits so well with the understanding of God proposed in this chapter. God, to be God, must create. The creative process is the very process in which God comes to know who God is, and that occurs through the growth and development of the created world. So, there is a duality in the evolution of the world and the growth of divine consciousness. There is a purpose to it all – the growth of consciousness both in the world and also as a consequence in God.

Better to be a live participant and contributor to the process than an inanimate watch!

Some Quick Questions

1. A Personal Nature.

When I ask whether God is personal, the answer is clearly "Yes." We are personal, i.e., think and will and more importantly have conscious loving relationships with other conscious beings, and therefore so must God who has made this particular possibility actual. And then there is the faith experiences that get the whole inquiry rolling. I don't have visions. Nobody appears at my bedside in the middle of the night to give me a message except my dog whining to go out. But there are occasions when there is more than distant silence.

Several years ago Kathleen and I went to a conference for professional people held in the hill country west of San Antonio. The lodge was located above a canyon through which flowed the Frio River. One afternoon I took a walk up the canyon beside the river. It was a time of depression about myself and the world in which I lived. I was fearful, almost unable to function. Life at best was just going through the forms.

It was a cool day, the sky startlingly blue above, the trees mostly leafless. Suddenly a breeze stirred the few remaining leaves and small birds flew overhead in a sudden flutter of wings. Something about sparrows and God's care lest a single one fall to the ground flashed in my mind. And deep within a flood of warmth rose overwhelming the fear and despair. At that moment I knew that there was something more than silence and darkness. There was comfort and hope and the ability to push ahead was suddenly present and overwhelming. Not a solid proof of the existence of a personal God. But sufficient, I thought, quite sufficient for me.

2. Pantheism.

Once I was talking about some of my ideas to a small circle of students. One, with a look of frozen concern, said it sounded like pantheism. Well, what about pantheism, long time bugaboo for all those emphasizing union with God and the closeness of God to creation? The short and simple answer is that there is no pantheism here in the sense that God and creation are essentially identified. The creative process requires a distancing of the created from the creator. The creator learns nothing about the creative self if what is created is simply the same as the creator. There must be some objectification, a standing apart and away from what is created if there is to be a growth in self-knowledge. I am not my children, I am not my thoughts. God is not the things that are created. But it all still remains clothed in mystery, for despite all the difference, there is an underlying unity that ultimately transcends all differences.

3. Trinity.

And what about the Trinity, that specifically Christian contribution to monotheism? I confess that I am not much interested in this complicated, esoteric belief. It is more than enough to try and come to grips with statements about the one God and that God's creation. But I think the model of creative activity can give rise to some thoughts along Trinitarian lines. In creating, the creator obtains an idea of self. Like all ideas it is other than the mind of the creator.

I might think of the first person as creative energy and the second person as God's idea or word about creative energy (reminiscent of the start of John's Gospel). And the third person might be the relationship of love flowing between creative force and self-knowledge or word – God's self-esteem, perhaps, to pick up a popular term. But I hesitate to go down this path. My lack of interest may simply be a defense mechanism. After all the years of studies in traditional theology, I am a little gun shy when it comes to left brain extensions of models. I've found I like better staying with the model and the story.

4. Omega Point.

Is there a clear point in the future where all converges, where God and God's creation are finally united and time comes to an end? Pierre Teilhard de Chardin, the Jesuit paleontologist thought so and he was one of my earliest heroic thinkers. God's potentiality is limitless, so it is at least possible that many universes existed before this one and many will after this one has come and gone. The scientific proponents of the Big Bang don't know whether this world will continue to expand forever or whether it will gradually slow, stop and collapse back upon itself in the Big End.

There is one very suggestive indication, however. Even agreeing with the evolutionists that evolution indicates that there is no such thing as design, there is ample evidence that the universe has moved from complete simplicity to astonishing complexity. Quite possibly this is because more complex things, if complex in just the right way for the time and place, have greater survival value than the less complex. The admission of purpose, in the sense of a drive or a push, as opposed to preconceived intent or design, seems not only possible but even likely. Perhaps, as some say, the next great evolutionary leap is away from adaptation of bodies and into adaptation of thoughts.

If there is an Omega Point, I do not think it will be an end but rather the point from which God and God's creation can grow together in understanding and love, without conflict and without end.

5. He or She.

One more point. I don't think God is either male or female. God the creator is both, containing within the possibility of both male and female. But, after millennia of patriarchal societies talking about God as Him and Father, I think it's just fine that the balance is being tilted a little back towards center by using Her and Mother. She can take care of Herself, but even God may appreciate a little help from Her friends.

Is This Really True?

Is God really and truly evolving? The answer has to be that I don't know. God is the ultimate mystery, greater than the mystery of our selves, which comes in second. But I think talking about God as limitless possibility, creating manifestations of that possibility and learning through the process, is a better way of talking than what I learned many years ago. The God I picture now is a God consistent with a creation that evolves and that has a certain, perhaps large amount of indeterminacy built in. When the world appeared static, we thought of God as static. An evolving world suggests an evolving God.

Perhaps somewhat strangely, this God is one who sounds a bit like the God found in the Old Testament, a God who was on occasion loving, angry, frustrated and patient. Then again, maybe not so strange. The writers of the Old Testament were looking at the historic experience of the Jews for their model, not at Greek philosophy. It's the picture of God built upon Greek philosophy and found in medieval theology, at least as it has been popularized, that causes the problems and that makes an evolving God seem so strange.

If the thinkers who put their mark on Christianity had gone back to Heraclitus, the story might have been different. He thought everything was in flux. You can't ever go in the same river twice – both you and the river change from one moment to the next. It's not even clear if you can go into the same river once! Where is Heraclitus now that we need him?

Still, it's all a theory, one that will doubtless change with the changes in experience that are relentlessly bound to come. I am finally reduced to plunging into the mystery of my experience of God in the hope that some illumination will well up out of that experience. For all our desire to talk and theorize, we are finally reduced to silence. Perhaps the best that can be said was the conclusion I heard John Courtney Murray gave to his final lecture on the subject of the nature of God. He had talked about the Trinity and the Incarnation and the Beatific Vision and ended stating: "Thus we find the darkness of one mystery illuminating the darkness of another mystery."

As Gawd said, it ain't no bed of roses.

CHAPTER FOUR

Diamonds in the Rough

"Let him who is without sin among you be the first to throw a stone at her" . . .
Jesus looked up and said to her, "Woman, where are they? Has no one condemned you?
. . . Neither do I condemn you; go, and do not sin again."

– John 8:7-11

Distrust all in whom the impulse to punish is powerful.

– Friedrich Nietzsche, *Thus Spake Zarathrustra*

Sin is whatever obscures the soul.

– Andre Gide, *La Symphonie Pastorale*

He said he was against it.

– President Calvin Coolidge,
on being asked what a clergyman
preaching on sin had said

Certain incidents came up through memory and, with them, the sudden falling away feeling in my stomach, as if an aching void had appeared somewhere between my lungs and my legs. At one time, I thought it was about when I was three-and-a-half years old, we lived in a first-floor apartment in a large stone house. I was still sleeping in my crib, which was set up in a corner of the bedroom. The house was heated by a large furnace in the basement; hot air rising from the furnace was fed through large pipes to openings in the floor of each room. These openings were covered by black grates, one of which was located underneath my crib. I could still remember my fear each night as I went to bed. Something was going to come up out of the grate. It would flow up around the crib and come in upon me. As I lay in the darkness, I would turn towards the wall and cover my head with the thin blanket, waiting fearfully for evil to arrive, until I finally went to sleep. I told my parents about this fear once, but they laughed and said there was nothing there and that I shouldn't think about it. So I did not mention it again.

The News from Eden

Genesis is a real blockbuster double feature. Hard on the heels of the story of creation comes the story of sin, shame and departure from the Garden of Eden. It's a marvelous story – trees of life and the knowledge of good and evil, tasty but unnamed fruit (the apple idea came along later), walks with God in the cool of the evening, talking serpents, leaves covering nakedness, cherubim guarding the gates (after the horse was stolen) with fiery swords. There's everything a great story ought to have and nothing it shouldn't have. Long ago I saw a cartoon showing a movie director stooping down and pointing a finger at a tiny item buried in a vast pile of food and drink, yelling: "What's coleslaw doing at an orgy?" The director would have been happy. There's nothing out of place in the story of the Garden of Eden.

Our problem with the great mythic origin tales is that we have ceased reading them as stories containing insights into what has made us the way we are. Our obsessive left brains start working to clarify, to pin down meanings, to wrap the insights up in transparent plastic and mass produce them, all sanitized and standardized. The ecclesiastical equivalent of the federal Food and Drug Administration has been around for a long time. Like all bureaucracies, it is more concerned about reducing the story to rules and regulations than hearing the story on its own terms.

So, what has often emerged from this great story are statements about original sin being a stain or blot on the soul of each new person from the moment of its conception, some horrible and intrinsic defect that places each of us in a primordial state of depravity. Protestant Christians have historically emphasized the depth of the depravity. Catholic Christians have insisted that human nature remains intrinsically good, but fallen forever from the better-than-natural state of its origin. In practice there doesn't seem to be much difference.

Joseph Sittler, my dissertation director at the University of Chicago Divinity School, once told me that he knew there was no real disagreement among Christians on the meaning of the Eucharist, despite all the obvious and clear differences in the official theologies of the different Christian churches. Everybody, he observed, walks back from receiving the bread and wine "looking like whipped dogs." Same thing when people talk about original sin. They start acting as if they had a great big "OS" branded for all to see on their foreheads. Adam and Eve were guilty and so are we. Shame is our birthright. We're no damn good. There's a bogeyman under the bed and he's going to get us. Paralyzed by fear, we stop even trying to be our own best selves.

Unless you are able to close your mind and your eyes, there are problems with this idea. First, if you take evolution at all seriously, there was no Adam and no Eve immediately formed just like the people next door, all ready and willing to make moral decisions. Recent discoveries have pushed the threshold of our earliest hominid ancestors back beyond four million years. Located in east Africa, these early ancestors of ours lived in a way not

greatly different from the chimpanzees. Life must have
been brutish, short, and indescribably difficult. The valley
where our first ancestors walked may have been wetter,
greener and cooler that it is now, but there is no evidence
of any Garden of Eden. If they walked in the cool of the
evening with God, it was nothing more (and nothing less)
than the walk we still take, the relationship with the
ground of our selves and all that surrounds us. But almost
entirely it was just the continuing struggle to respond as
adequately as possible to the surrounding world. The barest rudiments of conscious self awareness were present.
It flies in the face of all that we know to think that these
earliest ancestors committed or even had the capacity to
commit any act so wrong as to forever alter the condition
of all their progeny.

Second, those remote ancestors were the products
of a process that makes more mistakes and false turns
than right ones. The process involved an ongoing inter-
action between individuals and species and the environment around them. Their ability to do this successfully
determined whether they would or would not survive from
one generation to the next. So, in the long course of time,
everything had to be tried. That fruit might be poisonous
was one of their occupational risks. The only way they
could distinguish the good from the bad was by trial and
error.

We can call them the original sinners, if we want.
But I think it's closer to the fact to call them original
diamonds in the rough.

The world in which our ancestors lived, however,
was not a Catch-22 universe. They and we were not pun-
ished for doing what they had to do in order to survive.
They did, indeed, have to live with their consequences of
their actions, just as we do. But all the evidence indicates
that the consequences were of the same order as we still
encounter, not banishment forever from a golden resort.
Just opportunities missed, desires unfulfilled, relation-

ships destroyed, growth unachieved. And an occasional step forward on the long evolutionary journey.

The Genesis story about Adam and Eve eating the fruit of the tree of good and evil is not about shame or stains on our souls or even about punishment. It's a story about the way things were and are. If I have to reduce it to a few clear ideas (and I still find this useful from time to time, despite a growing desire simply point to the story without further words), I think there are three essential points, elements of the story that come through naturally and forcefully.

l. *Things are screwed up.*

The story of Adam and Eve, the serpent and the tree is an acknowledgment of something that must be clear to anyone who takes a good look around. Life and each of us is not ideal It's not a perfect world. No matter what I do, the result has a worm in it. There may possibly be a golden age, a Garden of Eden in the future, but there was none there at the beginning of human consciousness. It may be natural for societies who think the world is static to picture a primitive golden age from which the present has sadly fallen. But in a changing world, we are led to see ourselves and the world about us as simply embedded in a comedy or tragedy of errors.

Carl Jung tells us about the shadow – the dark side of our selves which we repress and from which we try to hide. What Genesis tells us about is that same shadow. I'm not OK, you're not OK, nothing's OK. But that, as somebody once said, is OK. Or it is once you come around to recognizing and acknowledging that none of us is ever free from our shadow world.

2. *Each of us is an active participant in the mess.*

Adam and Eve (taken as symbols of our earliest ancestors) were bound to screw things up during the course of their lives. Shit, as the bumper sticker says, happens, and Adam and Even were no exceptions to the rule. It didn't, however, just *happen* to them, just as it doesn't just happen to us. We are active participants in the process, not passive bystanders occasionally splattered with mud cast up by others. It's part of being alive, and none of us can escape it. We do, as the General Confession says, the things we should not have done and we fail to do the things we should have done.

3. Passing the buck.

Listen to Genesis. When God asks Adam what happened, Adam says: "The woman whom thou gavest to be with me, she gave me fruit of the tree, and I ate." Eve is certainly to blame and maybe God, too, since God was the giver of obviously flawed goods! And Eve, when also asked, says: "The serpent beguiled me, and I ate." It is not recorded what the serpent said. It probably came from a severely dysfunctional pit where it had suffered snake abuse and fang envy during its youth.

"The root of all disturbance . . . is that no one will blame himself." (Dorotheus of Gaza, a sixth century monk, quoted in Kathleen Norris, *Dakota: A Spiritual Geography*). Blaming something or somebody else may be our favorite move in the game of life. One of my most cherished examples of the tendency is the theory advanced by the bankrupt debtor who claimed damages because, he said, his bank was in the business of evaluating risks, should have known he was not credit worthy and therefore should not have lent him the money which had permitted him to ruin his business. Stop the world, we need to get off! I sometimes think that the popular interpretation of the Genesis acknowledgment of the way things are is itself a result of our great talent for passing the buck. How convenient for us to have a lead-footed ancestor who blew away paradise! We never had a chance. The whole human race comes from a dysfunctional family of origin.

Still, I don't think blame is quite the right word, whether applied to me or to you or to Adam and Eve. Blame should just mean responsibility, but it carries along with the idea of responsibility a dark cloud of evil nature and depravity. Taking responsibility is an empowering act. It implies that we could have done and still can do otherwise. Blame just sits heavy on our shoulders, pressing us further into the mire. Insight into the way things are should free us, not tighten our chains.

Revenge of the Pharisees

The popular notion of original sin as a single act of disobedience condemning us all to a sinful life and separation from God can create within us a sense of fear, shame and hopelessness that prevents us from seeing both ourselves and the world as they really are. When coupled with the popular understanding of salvation as flowing from the single act of Jesus' crucifixion, you can get a lethal brew. Alternately hung over and inebriated, we can spend a lifetime in a manic depressive state where we move from the depths of despair to the highest exaltation without ever touching firm ground.

Whatever the source of the problem, one thing is clear. The history of Christianity is a history of judgment, condemnation, religious crusades and persecution. We were lost but now are saved, you others are lost – and guilty, too. Not to worry, we'll see that you are "saved," like it or not. I once heard the president of a Catholic college say that the goal of her school was to force its students to be free. It was the authentic voice of a side of Christianity that is obsessed with control and judgment of everyone and everything it contacts. The voice of those who despised and fought Jesus lives on in the voices of all those who think it their duty to control the lives of others and to condemn all who do not follow the rules and regulations. "They bind heavy burdens, hard to bear, and lay them on men's shoulders; but they themselves will not move them with their finger." (Matthew, 23: 4). Call it the revenge of the Pharisees.

One other thing is clear. This world of control and judgment is not the world of the four gospels, those records of what the early Christian community remembered and thought about Jesus. The story told in the first part of the eighth chapter of John's Gospel gives a much different picture of how to deal with sin and judgment. The story is not found in all versions of the Gospel, but appears nonetheless to be an authentic incident in Jesus' life. I think it quite possible it was omitted by some collectors of stories about Jesus because it is so shockingly contrary both to the standards of his day and our own impulses. By a kind of intuitive contrarian way of dealing with what Jesus probably said and did, I am much inclined to give the story great authority. Jesus wasn't crucified for nothing – and this story is full of things that must have driven the Pharisees up the wall.

It is the story of a woman found committing adultery. The punishment, according to custom and the Law, was a ritual stoning by the upright. Jesus simply says that the first stone should be cast by one without sin. No stones are cast and the condemnors depart, one by one. Finally Jesus asks the woman if none are left to condemn her. When she says no one, he says that neither will he condemn her. How could this be? Is Jesus not, in the traditional understanding, himself without sin? Should he not, therefore, be the very one most able to condemn with all the outrage and righteousness of an angry God?

But he does not condemn. He refuses to engage in the blame game, to establish his own rectitude by finding fault in others. He does indeed say to the woman that she should sin no more. The refusal to condemn is not a statement that there has been no failure on the woman's part to do what she should have done. Acknowledgment of fault, on the part of both the woman and Jesus, is not at all the same as judgment and condemnation, the casting of another down in order that I, by comparison, be lifted up. Acknowledgment of fault provides an opportunity for metanoia, a change of heart and mind leading to growth and renewal. Judgment and condemnation recreate the world of the Pharisees, a bitter world of anger and death, without love and without hope.

When I encounter anger, judgment and condemnation, I know I am not in contact with anything coming from God. It is, instead, the voice of the Pharisees, still alive and well, even thriving, nearly 2,000 years after Jesus refused to condemn the woman taken in adultery.

Plans and Calls

I sometimes think of a woman I met at a church I was attending several yeas ago. She and I were both in a group studying one of the gospels. Her goal, made clear in one way or another over the course of weeks, was to find out what God wanted her to do with her life. She was convinced that God had a very clear and distinct plan for her, a path with all the turns and crossroads clearly marked with arrows and signs carrying the divine directions. Her problem was that she had thus far been unable to find either the path or the signposts. She continued, however, to search.

Our study group proved not very helpful. The rest of us were using the text as an opportunity for free association with what was going on in our lives, thinking we might find ways of understanding who we were and what we were doing. The times we spent together were, for most of us, exciting and surprising. We never quite knew what might turn up on any given Sunday, but we were rarely disappointed in our expectation that some light and warmth would enter our lives. We found attitudes and hints and shared our failures and our occasional successes. But we did not find any clear plans. The woman seeking God's plan for her soon dropped out.

Sympathy with a person seeking a clear and concise plan came easily, because I was obsessed with such a search for many years. When I was growing up in the eastern part of the United States in what I now know was a fascinating family relic of the Victorian Age, I thought I lived in a world where everyone but me knew how to act and what to do. My father, the son of a very proper, very distant man whom I never saw without coat and tie (and a vest once the weather had grown cool) and a domineering mother, had few ways of approving but many ways of condemning. The worst thing he could say about someone was that the person "didn't know how to act."

After his funeral those of us who had known him best and longest spent an idle hour talking about what might be put on his tombstone that could, in five or six words or so, sum up his life. The front runners were "He did it his way" and "He knew how to act." As it turned out, the tombstone selected when my mother died (and on which were chiseled under her name the words "The only stone she left unturned") did not have sufficient space for anything but his dates of birth and death. He selected the tombstone when my mother died. I don't know whether he consciously thought of any epitaph for himself. If he had, it would have been like him to leave no space for out of control comments by others.

There were intricate rules for everything. It wasn't just forks and spoons and butter knives. There were even rules for making and refusing or accepting invitations. People who knew how to act always repeated an invitation that they really meant at least three times. If they only asked you twice, they really did not want you to come; they were simply being polite. (It remains a mystery to me why it was thought polite to say something you didn't mean,) The invitee, on the other hand, was expected to refuse every invitation at least twice, in order to provide the invitation giver the opportunity to show that the invitation was genuine, or to get out before being taken up. Of course there were rules for whether you should finally accept an invitation – there were the right people and the right places and the right activities. And then there were all the dreaded wrong ones. The first list was rather short, the second quite long.

When I went to University of Chicago in 1967, I encountered a different way of dealing with the, to me, rule-laden subject of invitations. It was simple. You got asked once, and only if it was desired that you come. You had one shot to accept or refuse. I missed out on a lot of things I really wanted to attend before I caught on. I wasn't dealing with boors unaware of the basic rules of formal politeness, just with honest people who had the heretofore unexperienced habit of expecting honesty in return. A healthy hint; I should have taken it more seriously.

The feeling of not knowing the rules was sometimes a source of shame and nearly always of anger. Despite the anger, which should have been an early warning alarm, I continued for many dreary years to quest for the right way to act in every and all circumstances. It involved much thought and planning, and drove me and everyone around me to distraction. I could not take even a family trip (perhaps most of all a family trip, since that was something important!) without planning everything to the last detail – where we would stay, how many beds, lower or upper floor – nothing was left to chance if I could help it. The vacations were routinely awful. Reality in the form of accident or chance kept intruding, upsetting the plans. I was furious with everybody. But most of all I hated myself for one more clear failure to get it all right.

Just once we actually had a good time. In a rare moment when experience triumphed over neurosis, I handed Kathleen the job of obtaining accommodations for the vacation trip. Neither she nor any of us were ever sure of what the end of the day would bring. It was always a surprise, almost always a wonderful surprise. And we had fun laughing about the previous night and anticipating the next. I found myself enjoying it. Like that mid-western plain speech, it was another opportunity calling for a look at what I had been doing to myself and others, asking whether imaginary rules of engagement had anything to do with life. But the voice saying I was living in a prison of my own creation was still a wee, small one. I needed a little thunder.

Old habits die hard. My dry and barren landscape slowly, however, began to find silver linings in the thunderclouds that passed over it. The deaths of my parents provided unexpected insights. For as long as I can remember, my mother wanted to travel. She wanted to see the world and was forever planning where should would go when my father retired and they had enough money. She died when she was 73 without every having taken any of the trips of her dreams. Another opportunity to learn from experience: no matter how many years you live, life is very short if you always postpone the things you want to do. There's a lot to be said for eating dessert first. Break the rules. Have chocolate cake or pie for breakfast. Dinner may never come.

My father lived until he was almost 87. He died lonely, bitter and sad, a man whose ability to control events failed long before his desire to do so. Highly intelligent, exciting and pleasant to be with when he wanted to be, he missed most of the joy and love that life can bring when you give it a chance. He rarely did; controlling others was his Holy Grail. Once I heard him screaming at his housekeeper because she took the "wrong" way out of a shopping center parking lot. The "right" way was about 100 yards up the street. Another lesson: give up control and let things happen. You may not live any longer, but you won't feel as old.

The lessons may finally be having an effect. We have our house for sale. Past sales have always been nerve jarring experiences. But I am enjoying this one. I'm not planning in great detail how we will close an imagined sale, where the proceeds will be parked while we look for a new house, how much we will pay, how much we will borrow, from whom, at what rate of interest, with what reserve for taxes and insurance. We haven't decided what city we will live in next, let alone what house. Suddenly I find it fun to play around with it. Maybe a buyer will come today, maybe not. Whatever, I'm not disappointed in the world or myself. Just enjoying the wait. Something interesting will happen, sooner or later.

Of course that's on the good days. On the bad ones the demons still rise up from somewhere below the stomach. But they are getting thinner, have less energy. I don't think they will ever completely fade away. In fact, I hope they won't. I know they are a part of me and I don't want to lose them entirely. It is possible that I am at last starting to enjoy them. I'd better – they are also a part of life.

Looking back, I know I spent a vast amount of time trying to find my version of a divine plan. Impelled by the vision of something out there that I would fit into if I could just find what it was, I studied and taught and monked and lawyered. I don't regret any of those times in my life – I learned much from each of them. But I do regret the obsessions and the efforts at control and the shame I felt as each new ship ran aground on the rocks of the real world. We only have one shot at this world. It shouldn't be spent looking for something that isn't there, when there is so much that is there, wonderful, surprising, unanticipated, joyful. One track minds are a disaster in a trackless world where joy is available for all who have the ability not to seek it but to let go and relax into it.

A little planning can be a helpful thing – planning in the sense of things that we look forward to and that we make the minimum effort necessary so that they can happen. But planning that gets in the way of the unexpected events that inevitably come up and add so much to our lives is a very bad thing. Reality is always richer than we imagine it to be. So, I try now to live lightly, keeping my eyes open for the unexpected. The last years of my life may be richer than all that went before. I'm not, however, making any plans.

I no longer think that God has a plan for me or for anyone else. What I do think God has built into each of us is a call. Not a call from God to do something in particular. It is a call, instead, from within ourselves and from the world around us. Find who you are by going inside. Give up the "How To" manuals and look at your experience. Pay attention to what you have unexpectedly delighted in, what you have instinctively shunned. Hear the voices within that speak when you are silent. My dentist has a list of good things to do posted on the ceiling of the room where I recline in the chair while my teeth are cleaned. Drink champagne for no reason at all. Call a friend. Walk on the beach. Watch a sunset. It can all be summed up in one rule: get involved in today. Get a life.

What's In a Name?

A rose by any other name, Shakespeare said, would smell as sweet. Is it pointless, then, to use new names for old actions and events? Maybe not. Our understanding can become bogged down, clouded and confused when words take on too much baggage. The word "sin" has an extraordinary amount of baggage. Each age has focused on a particular problem and shoveled massive chunks of that problem into its picture of sin. The early Christian communities had a big problem with sacrificing to idols. The New England Puritans were obsessive about hypocrisy and backbiting. Our own time, still captive to the Victorians either as prisoner or rebel, can't get away from sex. *Webster's Third New International Dictionary* defines the verb as to "commit an offense against God" and then gives fornication as an example. A priest friend complains that he's sick of all the talk about penises and vaginas and their misuse.

We might give some thought to placing a moratorium on the word "sin." Not on the reality – that can take care of itself. Just on the word, so that we have a fighting chance of looking with fresh eyes at the reality.

After my stint at real estate law I moved to another law firm and began practicing in the area of corporations and partnerships and business transactions. I didn't do any work in the courthouse, except occasionally file some papers with the county clerk. The exciting, roller coaster world of trial lawyers was something I watched with fascination but without active participation. It was not until I started acting as a mediator of legal disputes that I really became aware of the great world of "torts" – injuries to person and property – that keeps the courtroom busy and the trial lawyers hustling.

The vast bulk of injury cases are those that are caused by someone's negligence. You've been negligent when you are dealing with somebody or something that you have an obligation to be careful with, and you fail to take that care. Driving down the street you don't see the red light, drive through and hit another car. Somebody is injured, at least their car is, and you are asked to pay for the damages. (In fact, if, like most, you have insurance, your insurance company is asked to pay. In one of the quainter anomalies of our legal system, we pretend in the courtroom that there is no such thing as insurance.) It is the essence of the idea of negligence that you have done an injury, that you are responsible for doing the injury, *but you were not aware of doing anything wrong until after the fact.* If you were aware of the wrong you were doing and deliberately went ahead anyway, it would be an intentional tort, and probably a crime as well. That's a very different bowl of cherries.

It took me a while to make the connection between the legal world and the world of moral fault, of sin. One happy day, however, it struck me that negligence is a good model of what happens most of the time when we commit what are called sins. We are incomplete, imperfect, struggling to find our way, have bad hair days, screw things up. Most of the sinful acts we commit are in fact nothing more than the moral equivalent of negligence – moral "mistakes." We are responsible for them (have "liability" in the legal world), but we didn't intend to do them, wouldn't have done them if we had been paying better attention or had been less clumsy. It's our fault, but our fault is not intentional, just part of the drama of being human.

Sometimes in a mediation the defending party is hung up on the whole idea of any mistake or fault on their part. It is as if they are unable or unwilling to deal with imperfection. As a mediator I know no settlement will be reached until we get past this problem. The mediation process works to help them see the whole situation through the eyes of others. Hearing the story from a plaintiff sitting on the other side of the table is often enough to break the logjam. In a few cases the defendant is simply unable to conceive that anyone could possibly find any fault in their conduct. There is no settlement and the case goes to the court house. I was interested enough in one of these hard cases to attend part of the trial. The jury did for the defendant what he was unable to do for himself – found him negligent. Not quite as negligent as the plaintiff had hoped, but negligent nonetheless. It was one of those situations where everybody, winner and loser, left the court unhappy.

Most of the time, however, defendants are able to acknowledge that their actions may have been just a wee bit shy of perfection. Once that hurdle is passed, it is much easier to move on to the question of damages. There is a nearly universal recognition that if you do something you should have avoided, you are responsible for taking care of the injured party. It's not as if you were being accused of sin. Or is it?

Over the ages we've put a lot of time and effort into particular sins. And we've put even more effort into flagellating ourselves about our supposed depravity. I can't recall ever having encountered anybody that seemed to me truly depraved. Maybe I've been extraordinarily sheltered or very lucky. But I've met a lot of people in the past 60 years. As for my record on luck, if Wall Street would base its predictions on doing the opposite of whatever I choose to do, we'd never have any losing days in the stock market.

I haven't met anyone free of moral negligence, either. Much of what we call sin and berate ourselves for is nothing more than a kind of negligence in the moral area. The real emphasis, as in the legal area, is the acknowledgment of our responsibility even when we have a million excuses for our action or lack of action. We should have done better. We didn't. We need to recognize it, make such amends as are possible, and get on with our lives.

When good men and women talk about their sinfulness, they are talking mostly about moral negligence. They know, as we often do not, that each person, no matter how closely united with God, remains an imperfect human being, rough edges and warts and all. We have to work at committing random acts of loving kindness. We commit random acts of moral negligence every day of our lives without any effort at all. It's part of the human territory. The saints know it and acknowledge it without fear or shame. Imitation of the saints, those especially radiant persons in our lives, remains a good idea.

Refusal to Grow

It's not all negligence, however, not in the legal world, not in the moral world. There are also those acts in which we have moved intentionally. In its popular conception, Christianity preaches a multitude of sins, all being committed with profligate frequency. It's an oppressive, frightening and shaming picture, perhaps the reason so many have fled their traditions. If fact, although moral mistakes are frequent, intentional sins are relatively rare.

For years I was puzzled how we could ever commit a serious sin. Nobody, I thought, did what they knew was bad for them. We're just like the animals in that respect – we do what we see as attractive to us; we don't do what we see as harmful or unattractive. Of course we (and animals) do things that are in fact harmful, but it's not known that way at the time. So how can those acts or omissions be sinful – don't you have to know what you're doing in order to be held morally accountable?

And what about all those "outside" influences? The environment, my family of origin, the terrible working conditions, and all the popular and faddish reasons why somebody should not be held responsible for an act – don't they excuse or explain anything bad I might do? Is it really true that to understand everything is to pardon everything? Yes and no.

I think of my own experience. Both of my parents were adult children of alcoholics. Raised in good Catholic families where divorce was unthinkable but the cruel and unusual emotional and mental punishment of family members was not, they imbibed the morality of self hatred, condemnation and control. They were also products of the great depression of the 1930s. It all had a tremendous impact on their lives and the way they thought about themselves and the world about them. In turn it had an impact on me. I, too, was an alcoholic. I, too, lived in the pattern of depression and self-loathing, through exaggerated expectations, then manic excitement over any expression of outside approval, only to ricochet back to hatred, disappointed anger and depression. As my father had before me, I tried to control my wife and my children and, in fact, the entire world with which I had contact. I yelled and raged and occasionally hit somebody. And I often felt that it was something over which I had no control.

But, if I had no control, a reedy voice kept whispering within, how could I be held accountable? The insane don't go to jail. Why should I go to hell? An asylum maybe, but not hell.

My life, I finally came to see through a series of opportunities that were pure gift, is more than the sum of its parts. By which I mean to say that you can't get to any answer on the question of responsibility if you pick each individual act out of the context of a life and try to determine whether the individual is fully responsible for that act. It's necessary to look at what the courts call "extenuating circumstances" – seeing an action in a broader context.

When I was finally able to step back from the particulars of my life and history, I was able to perceive an overall direction, and, more important, I was able to take responsibility for that direction. I don't think anyone gets to the point of being able to commit a really serious sin until they are standing at that kind of crossroads. We do indeed have the awful capacity to turn aside from light and peace and beauty. There is a "dark side of the force" within each of us which may fatally attract us. But there is also within us the bright side, the fundamental creative force that brought us into being and maintains our existence.

For some the choice may never come. Too overwhelmed by the demons within, they may never have the opportunity to make a fateful decision. For others, it may only come once in a lifetime. For still others, that kind of choice may be an opportunity repeated many times. Once made, it does not prevent our doing things we should not do, failing to do what we should, but a direction has been set. We move on an upward spiral or, if we turned to the dark, we move in a downward spiral. Make a choice of the light and it is suddenly one of those low humidity, bright clear days where the horizon seems open to the ends of creation. They may not come very often, but they make up for an awful lot of cloudy weather. But, choose the dark and suddenly you are caught in the unceasing whirlwind.

I find myself cherishing the definition of sin given by a fourth century Christian bishop, Gregory of Nyssa. Sin, he says, is a refusal to grow. As far as I now know, we human beings alone among all around us are called and have the ability to set the direction of our lives. Not bound to earth, we are called from within to acknowledge and then look beyond our moral negligence and the patterns of our lives. And we are called, too, from within to move from the seductions of the dark to the joys of light. To cease trying to reduce our sphere of imperfection, to refuse to open ourselves to our possibilities, these are both refusals to grow.

Mentors

Blame without shame, responsibility without fear, growth without death. It sounds impossible – and is if you stay on the left brain level, where only either/or exists and both/and has no place. It is a mystery, like God and creation. That very quality of mystery gives me some confidence I am on the right track. But how to see it concretely? What images can we call to mind?

An old friend is a New Testament scholar and teaches in a divinity school affiliated with other seminaries and divinity schools in the area. One of them, he tells me, recently offered a course titled "Animals as Spiritual Mentors." Visiting the campus bookstore shortly after publication of the course offerings, he saw a cat walk onto the premises. A student smiled and asked whether the cat was a new student. "No," my friend said, "one of the new faculty members." He reports the remark was not well received; it was not politically correct.

I'm not enough of a revolutionary to look for mentors in the academic curriculum. But there is something true in the thought of learning from animals. They carry the burden of being themselves better than we do, perhaps because for them it is not a burden. They are, they don't have to become. However natural and easy it may be for animals, there is an undeniable quality of grace under pressure that seems to characterize all their movements. Life is often short, rarely easy. But they move and act with a brightness of eye and a sureness of foot that belies imperfection and mistake.

Our dog Pookie is 14 or thereabouts – we don't quite know because she was given to us by people moving out of town when she was full grown. Arthritic, partly deaf and mostly blind now, she yet wags her tail as I come and go, loves her table scraps, takes her morning and evening strolls through the neighborhood, lies on the warm as-phalt in the middle of the street, goes about her life with a calmness and a steadiness that I can only envy. She is at ease with herself, centered in a way that we seek to discover, if we seek it at all, from gurus and expensive workshops.

We share 98% of our DNA with our closest relatives among the animals, the chimpanzees. We are animal bod-ies through and through. Our souls are not separate hu-man souls inhabiting an animal body for a brief period of time, waiting to be freed. They are animal souls through and through. Take that remaining 2% and add that we think as well as sense, will as well as respond by instinct. Can't we still achieve what animals achieve without thought – grace under pressure, intensity in a quiet still-ness?

I have been watching Ken Burns' documentary, *Base-ball,* as I puzzle about the reality of sin. It strikes me that the best of the ball players flitting across the screen have a quality of terrible intensity coupled with relaxed ease that permits them to make indescribable feats of planning and dexterity look as natural and dramatic as a cat stalking a bird. Baseball, a friend says, is the most human of our professional sports. Unlike football or basketball, where everything is supersized, baseball uses people who, even the best of them, look like us. Not to forget the New York Mets in their early years. They brought ineptitude to new depths and, in doing so, gave courage to all of us with two left feet. If it can happen in a game, why not in the whole of life? Maybe life is just the biggest game in town.

So, I make a note to spend more time watching animals and to attend ball games as often as possible.

* * * * *

The Ash Wednesday ritual reminds us: Remember you are dust and to dust you shall return. But we have the extraordinary power to make that dust shine as a star.

> This Jack, joke, poor potsherd, patch,
> matchwood, immortal diamond,
> Is immortal diamond.
> – Gerard Manley Hopkins, "No. 72. That Nature
>   Is a Heraclitean Fire and of the Comfort of the
>   Resurrection"

Well, yes, but still a diamond in the rough.

CHAPTER FIVE

The Book

Both read the Bible day and night,
But thou read'st black where I read white.
  – William Blake, "The Everlasting Gospel"

The Bible is literature, not dogma.
  – George Santayana, *The Ethics of Spinoza*

Who wants to be remembered by the notes of his students?
  – *The Hero's Journey: Joseph Campbell on His Life and Work*, ed. by Phil Cousineau

We sat in a circle, about a dozen of us, on folding metal chairs, the ones with a vinyl insert on the seat so they were only half as uncomfortable as they looked. The room was general purpose, cluttered with several desks and large tables shoved against the walls to make room for our group. Whenever the door opened we could hear conversation in the hall from those departing the just ended Sunday service. After a brief opening prayer one of the group read the passage from the Bible selected for this week's study.

Except we really didn't study. I was the group leader and had no pretensions to being a Scripture scholar. We did have notes to the text and some of us had even read both text and notes prior to the meeting. But mostly I assumed nothing, which was the reason why someone always read the week's passage at the beginning of the meeting. On any given Sunday, that was very probably the first contact with the text for some of the group members.

No one lectured. Instead an opportunity to speak moved around the room, sometimes in a circle to my left, sometimes to my right, my effort to discourage any inveterate back of the church folk from hiding. But it was always acceptable to pass the invitation to speak along to the next person. Getting started was the most difficult and those who passed were usually at the beginning. Often they offered comments later, once the talk was rolling.

Today's reading was on the marriage feast at Cana. A few comments about weddings, one or two about drinking. Then a woman, after hesitating, started to talk slowly about her mother and the tensions and strains between them. Her voice shook occasionally and she stopped completely once or twice. Her mother was dead and it was mostly a story of missed opportunities, chances to speak or act untaken. When she finished, others joined, some comforting, some telling similar stories, sharing experiences from their lives. Time for mourning, time for hope, time for simply remembering with others. No conclusions, but perhaps a lesson.

The hour came to an end swiftly. A brief closing prayer, and then the room emptied. Had anything or anyone been there besides ourselves?

The Mona Lisa's Smile

In *Dakota: A Spiritual Geography,* Kathleen Norris speaks vividly about her family history. One of my favorite characters, out of a family richly endowed with characters, was the grandmother who asked all comers, "Are you saved?" The question implies a lot. It surfaces in a belief system where God's choice of the elect is eternal and the elect themselves are a limited group. But it is a decision knowable by those among the elect. Whether possessed by a sudden phenomenon of being "born again" or steeped

in a slow boiling conviction, on the burner since childhood, the elect know they are saved.

I have from time to time encountered men and
women who talk of Jesus as if he were an intimate friend,
a regular visitor in their lives, a person with whom they
have an ongoing conversation. They have, they say, accepted Jesus, and it has changed their lives.

This has not happened to me. I have tried to imagine
what it would be like to know that I am saved or to have
Jesus as an intimate companion. But the assurance of
being saved is not there, and all that comes when I try to
imagine Jesus present is a ghostly image that looks all too
like the statues and paintings beloved by pietists and ro-
mantics of the nineteenth century. When the source of
an image intrudes into the mind, you know you're in
trouble! And then there have been the self-proclaimed
Christians telling me what they do has been commanded
by the Lord. Often as not the "commands" seem to include
relentless repression of spouses and children, grim oppression of employees or competitors. It is a religion with
which I am familiar, but not one in which I have any
desire for further participation.

In my experience, those who proclaim themselves
saved and intimates of Jesus have often been the very ones
I would least like to imitate. On the other hand, those
whom I have found the most loving, kindest and ethical
have mostly been the very ones who are least certain about
their ultimate place in God's kingdom, and have the least
knowledge about what Jesus is saying to them, if anything
at all. More often than not, the voices and lives of those
who quietly offer an attractive way are submerged and
drowned out by the babble of self righteous religious
barbarians. Unable to hear sufficient numbers of credible
contemporaries to tell me what Jesus is like, I am left with
the historical record, the New Testament section of the
Bible and all the commentaries and studies about it down
through the centuries.

My religious heritage, Roman Catholicism, makes a strong distinction between Scripture and Tradition. Scripture is the books of the Bible, the writings which came to be officially accepted by the Church in the second and third centuries, a long time after the death of Jesus. The beliefs of the Church about the meaning of these writings, and much more, is Tradition – what the believing community has determined it has heard in the course of its life.

Years ago, in the seminary, a quiet but intense argument engaged one of the professors of New Testament with one of the professors of theology. It was Scripture versus Tradition, and it had all the passion (but not quite the color) of a classic Notre Dame game. "What the Scripture said" was the battle cry of the New Testament man. "What the Church has heard" was the motto of the theology man. Long after the battle cries had faded, I realized that, in a sense, they were both correct. At the center of the arena *is* what the believing community has heard. And yet, the books of the Bible, like any writing, must be taken on their own terms, listened to for what is actually said and not for what we might like them to say.

In recognition of the need to hear what was said, over the past several centuries the Christian churches (Protestant first and then finally Catholic) have researched those books carefully, using modern historical methods and literary criticism as keys to unlocking what the scriptures say. What they have sought is to grasp the original meaning, to get a hold of what had been heard at the time the books were written and even earlier, back to the very moment when Jesus spoke and acted. An effort to feel the breeze as it first blew, to see the waves in the water before they reached the shore.

The picture of Jesus that emerges is not as clear as one might expect, given the time and effort put into the enterprise. The only thing that is reasonably clear, in fact, is that what has been called Tradition was at work from the very beginning. The four gospels appear at first glance to be eyewitness accounts. Looked at more closely, they clearly are not. Jesus' life was not a series of events surrounded by a swarm of breathless television reporters, cameras carefully recording every movement and every statement. Instead what we begin to see is the shadow of a figure moving about Palestine, teaching those about him, and particularly a small select group. After Jesus' death – exactly how long after is not clear – members of that initial group and others began to tell and then record certain things that Jesus said and did, but not now as immediate onlookers. Instead they were working out of memory, and then memories of memories, all influenced by the recognition and conviction that what Jesus had said and done was of extraordinary import.

As time passed the stories and sayings were collected and the gospels as we know them began to emerge, as well as other collections that did not make the final list of approved accounts. These writings were edited and formed in the cauldron of a growing community of believers, Jew and non-Jew alike, hardly any (and, in a short time, none) of whom were present with Jesus during his lifetime. From a strictly literal recollection (although even those efforts at literal recollection must have been subject to all the imperfections, tricks of memory and plain old wishful thinking that encumber "eyewitness" accounts), the emphasis inevitably moved to teaching and stressing what the writers believed and then the community accepted as what Jesus "really" meant. In short, the writers had gained a theological point of view, which the stories and sayings of Jesus illustrated. In the midst of this development, the points of view of the different authors diverged, depending on which audience they were writing for, with which strand of the accounts they were most familiar, and, of course, what their own faith experience had been.

Modern scholars of Scripture as well as today's seekers are left with a mixed bag of evidence. That there was a historical figure named Jesus, born and living in Palestine and then crucified sometime about the thirtieth year of his life, seems scarcely to be questioned. What kind of a person he was, what exactly he said and did, what he intended to teach is not nearly so clear and certain. There are almost as many different pictures of Jesus available today as there are scholarly writers, and perhaps as many as there are believers. Whether coming to Scripture as scholar or believer, each of us inevitably seeks the answers to the questions that have arisen in our lives, and in so doing, we with equal inevitability, shape the answers we hear.

There is, finally, little difference between Scripture and Tradition. Scripture itself is the written record formed by those who believed in Jesus during the first century or somewhat more after his death – the Tradition of those early believers. What we have come to call Tradition carries on the work of stating what later believers have heard, their hearing formed not only by careful reading of Scripture, but also by the events of their daily lives. The division between Scripture and Tradition begins to fade and disappear. It is a question of time and emphasis rather than any strict dividing line.

Still another complication. Surely, one might be inclined to think, there is a goal here. If all are trying to comprehend who Jesus was and what he meant and means, is there not a definitive historical reality towards which all interpretations, official Scripture as well as later Tradition, point? Can we not with more careful study come closer and closer, until, like that definite and knowable geometrical limit towards which the curve moves always closer but never touches, we are able to proclaim that "this" is who Jesus was, "this" is what he meant and means? Or at least, close enough?

But this assumes that Jesus himself was totally outside the process, that he knew precisely who he was and what he intended to teach from the very beginning. And this should make us careful. As both Scripture and Tradition insist, Jesus is at least fully human. Would he be so if he were exempt from all the normal process of growth and development? A man who knows himself to be god, with all the power and knowledge that would imply, may not be a man at all. The old idea that Jesus was just God in disguise rears its head. I hold on to the reality of his being fully human, and therefore cannot help but conclude that Jesus himself had to go through the process of coming to self understanding, just as we all do. He wasn't born with a set of Cliff notes giving him immediate access to eternal answers!

So, even were we able to conclude with complete certainty that certain words and actions were truly those of Jesus, we are still left with an area of cloud and mist. Who did Jesus think he was? What did Jesus intend – what was he trying to teach his contemporaries and, by extension, us? To use the words Winston Churchill once applied to Russia, it is as if Jesus were a riddle wrapped in a mystery inside an enigma. Better, the meaning of Jesus is like the Mona Lisa's smile. When you go to see the Mona Lisa, I read or was told, the Mona Lisa is not on trial, you are. It is the same with the life of Jesus. When Scripture is read, you are called to respond. But what is the response, and to what? What is that smile? What does Jesus really mean? Like all those who have gone before, even (perhaps most of all) those who walked with him through Galilee and the streets of Jerusalem, I have to find that meaning by attending to my own experience while I read the book.

Peripheral Vision

Scripture and Tradition stand in relation to the rest of my experience; they are not outside but themselves are experienced, changing and being changed in the course of the relationship. I face, however, a dilemma. Can I rely on what those who have studied and researched Scripture over the centuries have concluded? If I do, am I not just trying to walk in their shoes, in effect trying to take on the experiences and thoughts of times past? Even if the scholars are my contemporaries, is my experience the same as theirs? Is it enough to read what they write and accept the picture given – even if I can form a composite picture that is the result of all the different views offered?

Or must I undertake my own concentrated study? To do so means learning the ancient languages, studying the history of the Mediterranean world into which Jesus was born, infiltrating myself so deeply into the first century world that I can believe I am hearing directly and unedited the words of Jesus himself? I judge that task ultimately impossible, not just because of a lack of time and ability on my part, but also because the 19th-century historian's dream of uncovering what really happened is just that – a dream. None of us can become completely other selves, erasing our own experiences in order to be a fresh slate on which another time and place can make a timeless, unaltered mark.

There must, I sense, be another alternative.

I come to the Scriptures always with a question of some kind – is this God speaking or human responding? Who is this man Jesus? What did he really say? These or some other question are there at the start of the search, prodding me to look into the text. And, with the questions, I find myself always having some expectations. I have, after all, been raised as a Roman Catholic, studied in a seminary, listened to sermons for years. My background is a lush garden full of flowering plants and weeds, something from which I cannot ever fully escape whenever I encounter the landscape of Scripture.

The result of a walk through that landscape has often been disappointment. A voice cries within: Is this all there is? To find an expected answer may have some comfort value, but none at all of shock or amazement or astonishing joy.

But, sometimes there is something else. I identify its source as a kind of spiritual peripheral vision. When I keep to single vision, my eyes focused straight ahead, I see only what I am already prepared to see. But when I loosen the focus and allow attention to wander, then the opportunity is there for something to happen. A phrase, a brief description, something the focused eye had passed over often without seeing. Suddenly my attention shifts and I see for the first time what, behind the present question and the current expectation, I have really been seeking. There is a shock of recognition, as if I had always known what was there, but had never before been able to bring to the surface of my mind.

It happens only when I am ready to let go of the questions and expectations with which I started. It is not ridding myself of them entirely, just letting them go so that something else can slide into the place they occupied. To look backwards is to see a path already defined by previous choices. It is easy to extend it mentally into the future, that next step just a projection of the preceding ones. But that is not the way. The path of the past does not disappear, but the next step is not determined by that path unless I make it so. Instead of looking backwards, I look ahead and sideways, waiting for the shadow or the fleeting glimpse of a place to step. To find my life, I must always be prepared to lose it.

The Nefertiti Effect

In 1966 I was in Berlin, traveling with a friend after spending the first part of the summer studying German in Salzburg. We spent part of a day in the eastern zone visiting the museum containing the great altar from Pergamum. It fell on dead eyes. Perhaps the contrast between the still largely undestroyed remnant of a once great ancient civilization and the tattered remnants of the modern Third Reich just outside the museum door was too unnerving. We decided to try another museum and took the subway to Dahlem, a suburb of west Berlin. We had no particular idea of what we might find, and wandered from room to room without either great expectation or any disappointment. All interesting, cultural, good for the spirit, and a nice educational use of our minds and spirit.

We were about to take our customary bihourly break for a beer in the museum cafe when I turned into a small room, about 15 feet square. In the center on a pedestal rested the only object in the room – the bust of Nefertiti. Twenty-eight years later I can still remember the shock of recognition and the piercing thrill that the greatest works of art, no matter how old, no matter from whence they came, can create in the viewer. There was a timeless moment or a moment of eternity, when that painted and crowned face, perfection from any angle, spoke across the ages.

What I know about Egypt I learned mostly from *Aida*. No chance of my having grasped Nefertiti as an ancient Egyptian might have. I knew the significance of nothing, but somehow had caught a view of the meaning of everything. What if Scripture might be read that way, not as by a first century Christian or one from any other century but my own? Was it possible that a valid meaning could emerge from the text, even when read by someone oblivious to the theological intents of the various writers, the validity of sources, even the reverberations in the New Testament readily available to those, ancient or modern, familiar with the Old Testament?

We take it almost for granted that the art of other cultures is available to us if we will only take the time to look with open eyes or ears. But then we do not normally give great religious significance to works of art. Perhaps that is one of the mistakes of our time and place. Other cultures have found space for art in their places of religious worship, often the location of their greatest works of art. Today we look at ceremonial masks and totem poles and even Gothic cathedrals as secular objects. But the power is present and, if we have not already decided that any power other than the secular is only magic, we can experience it in something of its original state. What they called miracle, we want to call magic and dismiss it. But that is not necessary. It depends on how open and available we are willing to let ourselves be.

I think that explains how it was that one of the gospel narratives of Jesus' trial and death came across so powerfully when, discarding all the learned commentaries and refusing to look at the footnotes decorating the bottom of the pages, I read it through in 1967, the Thursday before Easter. The same thing was happening as our study group made its way Sunday after Sunday through one of the gospels. None of us became first century listeners to Jesus. We remained solidly in the 20th century, but we experienced a relationship with God that was here and now, not there and then. A different relationship, because we differ from our ancestors and because God, in relating to us here and now also differs from the divine being in relation to those people there and then. Yet I sense there remains a continuity that can be experienced, even if it is not only difficult but finally impossible to explain it adequately.

The scholarly study of Scripture has a value. It can give us further insights and enhance the ones we have already had. But it is not a substitute for that relationship that can emerge from contact with the Scripture by an open and ready reader. When the student is ready, an old eastern proverb says, the teacher appears. The Scripture appears when we are ready. For some that may involve deep study, for others it may be a gift as available as a sunny day. For all it is an event open to transcendence of both the past and the present.

If I were to put this into a more logical framework, it would be by stressing that God is everywhere and always in relation to the created world. That being the situation, God is as much in relation with us today as God was to those men and women in first century Palestine who first followed Jesus. The Scriptural record of the early community's reaction to Jesus is simply an occasion for us today to respond to the ongoing relationship of God to creation. Scripture is the record of how faith experience in the past has seen fit to talk about that faith. It is not the necessary way controlling our response. But it provides suggestions and may, if we are fortunate, lead us into a new or deeper experience of faith that we can, in turn, struggle to express in words suitable to our situation in time and space.

Why read the Christian Scriptures and attend to Christian Tradition at all, if the God relationship is present everywhere to all, regardless of whether they are even aware of the existence of the Christian Scriptures and Tradition? My reason is simply that the religion in which I have been nurtured and grown is the Christian religion, tracing its beliefs back to Jesus. Knowledge of what Jesus said and did is not necessary for the experience of union with God, but it is an opportunity, and a special one for me given my particular history.

I therefore work between two perimeters. On the one side is my faith experience of God in relationship to me. On the other side is the recorded response to Jesus of those who have found their faith experience in con-nection with Jesus or, in the contact with Jesus, had other faith experiences arising elsewhere confirmed or ex-panded. If I am to pay proper attention to my own back-ground, I will focus on the record of Jesus' acts and words, using it as a limit for my own statements of belief. If my statement of belief is to be within the framework of the Christian community, then it should show a connection with the words and acts of Jesus. At the risk of becoming a herniated believer, I stretch one foot back to the begin-ning, seeking some firm footing in Jesus' words and deeds, while placing the other foot squarely on all else in my own experience.

* * * * *

A last word, or a few last words, reminders to myself as much as to anyone else.

l. Don't be compelled to finish anything.

I used to feel I had to finish every book I started. And so, I spent or wasted a lot of time and energy reading badly written or badly thought books (usually both, bad writing goes hand in hand with bad thinking). Sometimes, the book was good, but I wasn't ready. In either case, I plodded on, finally able to say "Well, that's finished, at last." I've stopped doing that. If the book is bad, or merely seems bad to me because I am not ready for it, I stop. Experience won't be forced.

2. Don't set a schedule.

I've often thought I should take 15 or 30 minutes a day to read Scripture, starting with Genesis and working my way through to the final book of the New Testament, with all the apocryphal writings thrown in for good measure. Bad idea, for me at least. Again, it's a question of taking it when you're ready. It is a good idea to work at setting some time aside each day for meditation, and that may include some reading from Scripture. But not on schedule, and not book by book. In the middle ages, there was a custom of seeking the answers to problems by opening Scripture at random, fingering a passage with eyes closed, then opening the eyes to read. I don't think God guides our hands and fingers to an appropriate answer. But it is just possible something interesting can happen when we stop controlling the selection.

3. Don't read to confirm what you already think.

We spent a lot of time in the seminary using the Bible to provide proofs for what, through philosophical reasoning or weight of custom, we already thought was true. Scripture isn't a deposit of ore to be mined for its value in proving logical propositions. It is there to be read by itself, for itself. The only goal other than seeing and hearing the text itself is to move beyond the words into the experience of God the text attempts to convey. You can find anything you want in Scripture if your goal is to get a phrase or an event that "proves" whatever statement it is you want to prove. So, don't waste your time. Seek only the experience underlying the text.

4. Don't get bogged down in scholarly commentaries.

They are written by academics, whose occupational disease is enhanced inability to distinguish the trivial from the important. It will only feed into the inability of each of us to make that same distinction. Use them when you feel a need to get background and details on specific questions that have occurred to you while reading the text. Or read them sparingly for the overall approach and for the general conclusions. God can no doubt be found in the details, but I find God also easily lost there.

5. Disregard all of the above and do what works for you.

Use your instincts and do what seems right at the time. That may involve regular reading of Scripture for a period. It may call for some serious time with scholarly commentaries. Or it may call for getting out of the chair or off the kneeling pad and experiencing some more of the world outside your walls. After many years of obsessive behavior based on what I thought I ought to do as laid down by outside sources, I've finally learned (mostly, at least) that trusting instincts that rise from deep within is the only good policy. The founder of the Jesuits, St. Ignatius, spoke in his *Spiritual Exercises* about the discernment of spirits. The good spirits, I think, are our deepest instincts; the bad ones are all those other shallow impulses and ideas we pick up from outside.

The best advice I've ever received on this is that of Joseph Campbell: "Follow your bliss." Campbell's own life had its share of unexpected turns and twists. Mine has, too. Looking back, however, I see a recurring light. Whenever a major decision loomed, I always found it useful to wait for the moment of inner certainty. Like Supreme Court Justice Potter Stewart, who couldn't define pornography but knew it when he saw it, I was never able to define in advance the curve of the next turn in my path. But I knew it when I saw it – it provided an inner warmth and glow. You know your bliss when you come across it.

We can trust our instincts if our eyes and hearts are not closed. "You know how to interpret the appearance of earth and sky; but why do you not know how to interpret the present time?" (Luke 12:56).

CHAPTER SIX

The Man

Jesus loves me – this I know,
For the Bible tells me so.
> – Anna Bartlett Warner, "The Love of Jesus"

And here's to you, Mrs. Robinson,
Jesus loves you more than you will know.
> – Paul Simon, "Mrs. Robinson"

For the sake of your tradition, you have made void
the word of God.
> – Matthew 15:6

The divine lives of saviors are symbolic of the meaning of the savior's teaching.
> – *The Hero's Journey: Joseph Campbell on His Life and
> Work*, ed. by Phil Cousineau

*I was in Germany in 1991, in the Dorndorf region about 50
miles north of Frankfurt, visiting an Indian holy woman, Mother
Meera. She lived in Thalheim. We stayed at a neighboring village,
about a half mile away. In the evenings, we walked a narrow
path through the fields between the two villages. The whole area
was one of low rolling hills, wooded sections here and there, but
mostly fields. You could see two or three other villages, all within
a mile of each other, spread across the land.*

I thought of the Palestine in which Jesus lived. Except for the green – Palestine always comes up tan and dusty in my mental geography – I imagined the scene much the same as Dorndorf. A farming area, small villages spread across the landscape, each within easy walking distance. "Along the way" is one of Mark's common introductions to a Jesus story, and I imagined Jesus moving along a road, talking as he went to his followers, perhaps picking a stem of grain from the field as we did moving to Thalheim.

I see no flowing robes, no long hair, no beard. Instead a man not old so much as of a rare age for a time when less than 25 percent of the population reached 30. Clothed in a simple earth-colored tunic, belted at the waist, with sandals on his feet, he walks rapidly along the way, stopping now and again to speak to the men and the women following him, and to those who, hearing of his presence in advance, come out from the villages.

"What," I hear him ask, "do you come out to see?"

Jesus' Message

Jesus was a carpenter's son and probably himself a carpenter, growing up in a remote village in Palestine, a very remote and unimportant part of the Roman Empire. He was a man from the lowest class, without power or protectors of any kind – why would anyone conclude that there was something so extraordinary about Jesus that they would want to follow him, even after his death?

I assume he had a charismatic personality, the ability to affect those with whom he dealt so strongly that they would be immediately attracted to him. But every time and place has individuals whose personality is so striking that they attract a following. Out of sight, out of mind in the great majority of those cases, and in few or none is there a result as dramatic as in the case of Jesus and the group of followers that formed upon contact with him. Something much more must have been at work.

I have never seen Mother Teresa. The accounts of her suggest that she says little but does much. Her work with the poorest, most destitute of human beings speaks louder than any words she might utter. Jesus must have looked the same. What was at work was the life he lived and the message that life gave to those who followed him. Nothing else can account for the perseverance of the followers after his death and their ability to spread their own experience of faith. But what message?

Reading the four gospels, those writings giving the most immediate and direct account of the sayings and deeds of Jesus, the words and acts that reach out and speak to me are those that appear to have been most in conflict with the expectations of the time and place in which he appeared, and which continue to be in conflict with the expectations of our own time and place. I confess to an affinity for the unexpected and divergent. I'm infected with a deeply contrarian view – Jesus would not have upset the established order so much or attracted his followers so greatly had he not challenged the expectations of all, followers and opponents alike, to a new experience of the world and themselves. No teaching about the mere perfection or completion of the existing order could have had such an effect. Only a message that changed lives could have had the lasting impact we find in Jesus. If we want to stay as we are, we shouldn't look into Jesus.

But, as the history of the Christian churches attests, there are many messages found in the gospels and in the other books of the New Testament. From this multitude of possibilities, I turn to those that shout out their contrarian aspect. This is the kind of stuff I believe could and did provide the astonishment necessary to generate a faith experience in Jesus' contemporaries and succeeding generations.

1. Here and Now

My father always had a hard time concentrating on the present. I think he found it too full of flaws. So, he talked about a past where the pain was less or he looked ahead to something in the future. Mostly he looked ahead. There was always a list of trips and his days were filled with making plans. The future constantly intruded into the present, as if the future were more real than what was happening here and now. Kathleen and I were alternately irritated and amused. When we visited we could never quite cope with digging into a splendid dinner while being asked what we wanted for breakfast. Seemed the pleasure of the moment ought to be sufficient.

Ignoring the present in favor of a golden past or future is not limited to individuals. Cultures do the same thing. The Garden of Eden myth in the Old Testament implies a yearning for better times. So does all the New Testament talk about a final time when the kingdom of God will be established anew. To say nothing about all those golden buildings and golden streets in heaven found in popular imagination. Can you play golf in heaven? Would it be worth going there if you couldn't? It won't be like the present – no divots, the ball always clears the water and the sand traps, putts forever fall into the cup. A heaven after death and a final restoration of the golden kingdom is the future equivalent of the lost garden of Eden.

A future kingdom, however, is not what Jesus points to. Instead he insists on the presence of the kingdom *here and now.* "Being asked by the Pharisees when the kingdom of God was coming, he answered them, 'The kingdom of God is not coming with signs to be observed; nor will they say, "Lo, here it is!" or "There!" for behold, the kingdom of God is in the midst of you'" (Luke 17:20-21).

This is the one saying that corresponds most closely to my faith experience of God's present and continuing relationship with the world and all that is in it. It is not so much a matter that I do not care if God was present at the creation and will again be present at any final Omega point. My faith experience is about God's presence now. It does not call for or point to either a past or a future. If it tells me anything about past and future, it says that I cannot change what has happened and I do not know what will happen. But I am in immediate contact with the present time and place and I am directly aware that I have the opportunity to relate either positively or negatively to it. It is that same present that the Jesus I find in the New Testament calls me to see and to work within. The past, if it intrudes at all will only help me understand the present context within which I work; the future will take care of itself.

There are many statements in the Gospels, the "main line" collections of Jesus' sayings and deeds, that confirm this stress by Jesus on the here and now character of the connection with God. I find one of the best and most explicit in Matthew 25:35-40: "'For I was hungry and you gave me food, I was thirsty and you gave me drink, I was a stranger and you welcomed me, I was naked and you clothed me, I was in prison and you came to me.' Then the righteous will answer him, 'Lord, when did we see thee hungry and feed thee, or thirsty and give thee drink? . . . . 'And the King will answer them, 'Truly, I say to you, as you did it to one of the least of these my brethren, you did it to me.'"

I am connected (or disconnected) with God in the acts of my daily life. More, it is in the actions of my daily life that I have the opportunity to know God. Just as it says in John's first Epistle (1 John 4:7-8): "Beloved, let us love one another; for love is of God, and he who loves is born of God and knows God. He who does not love does not know God; for God is love." Whatever may come in the future, whatever has occurred in the past, human beings have the opportunity here and now to connect with God and to know God in that connection.

2. The Extent of Here and Now

When I visited my grandmother as a child, we had a choice of Catholic churches. There was Immaculate Conception, the "Irish" church, where my Irish grandfather had donated a pew which carried his name on a little brass plate. There was also St. Agnes, the "German" church (which somehow also included the Italians). My grandmother, descended from English and German immigrants, was even handed about all this ecclesiastical nationalism. So, when I stayed with her I attended the grade school at St. Agnes, which was closer, but we usually went to Mass at Immaculate Conception.

The town where my great grandmother (on Dad's side) lived was much smaller than the one where my grandmother lived. But it had three Catholic churches – the "Irish," the "Polish" and the "Slovak." At one time it had four – the last one perhaps for all those not blessed by birth into one of the other groups. I don't recall wondering about this situation – why or how the believers in Jesus and members of a "universal" church got segregated by nationality. Like the segregation that existed in Washington while I was going to Georgetown in the 1950s, it was something there, taken for granted, hardly noticeable.

In the last 40 years I've traveled a lot and read a lot and met a lot of people, different in race, religion and nationality. They are not ideas any longer, something that could be tucked into a corner and ignored. Surprise of surprises! The people, when I get down to it, seem a lot alike. Lots of differences but underneath it all a quality of being human that transcends race and religion and national origin. It's not easy to retain a Greek mind in all this. The Greeks called everyone but themselves "barbarians." But there these real people are and they aren't any more (or any less) barbaric than I and those I always thought of as "we" – my group, my folks.

That's the reality that Jesus saw and acted upon and taught. A community without boundaries – no "us" and "them," just a universal "we." Take the story of the Good Samaritan (Luke 10:29-37). A man travels from Jerusalem to Jericho. He is attacked by robbers, and left half dead by the side of the road. He is passed first by a priest and then by a lawyer, each an example of a class manifesting the old law and the old tradition. Neither stops. Along comes a Samaritan, a group of people with connections to the Jewish tradition but especially despised and looked down upon by those in the Jewish community because of their rejection of a portion of the "truth." He is the one who takes up the wounded man, delivers him to a place of refuge and healing, and provides for his care until he is well. This, Jesus says, is the neighbor. It is hard to imagine the shock this must have caused Jesus' audience. To get close, translate this by imagining one in the midst of the Cold War claiming that a man from Moscow is our neighbor.

Jesus pushes the message by curing the child of a Roman centurion. He goes outside Jewish territory to Greek cities across Lake Capernaum, east of Galilee. He acknowledges both the existence and rights of Caesar. It is not a world of us against them. He preaches instead a world where there is only us, all of us regardless of race or belief or color or nationality. There are no "thems" there. It was shocking then, and it is shocking now when we still live in a world of boundary disputes, historical enmities and let me get mine first lest you get yours before me.

Demanding and frightening as Jesus' proclamation of the kingdom spread among all is, I have to acknowledge that it is the only view that fits and conforms with my own faith experience. The faith experience is one of no boundaries, no limit to the spread of God as foundation of all that exists.

"No man is an island," John Donne wrote in the 17th century. Neither is any culture or group, not even the ultimate group of all human beings in all times and places, immersed in and saved from ultimate isolation by the sea of God.

3. The Price of Admission

I remember our oldest child, Sean, not yet able to walk but able to hold on to tables and shelves and chairs, moving from support to support around the room, picking up each ashtray, book, plant and whatever that came in his way, looking at each carefully before moving on (sometimes with sad results, as the day we found every potted plant in the dining room upside down on the floor).

And our second child, Colin, always 30 or 40 feet behind us as Kathleen and I took an evening walk, as if to say he did not want us to spoil his investigations by giving him ready answers. He picked up each pebble, explored each clump of grass, looked at every crack in the sidewalk, pulling in bits and pieces of experience like a vacuum cleaner. Then our third child, Megan, the fearless climber of trees, tenacious interrupter of her brother's games and quiet but deep observer of all around her.

Until frightened away by some adult warning, they were ever ready to look into anything, open anything, taste anything, try anything. Spontaneity, curiosity were their birthright and they exercised them fearlessly. Always open to anything new, they took everything on its own terms. How could they do otherwise, since they did not yet have the adult stock of prejudices and denials, that acquired ability to ignore what is here and now in favor of some learned "correct" behavior or attitude?

Love, if we take Jesus' life and teaching seriously, can be called the admission ticket to the kingdom. The central role of love is confirmed in Jesus' reply to the question of which commandment is primary. Jesus reply (Mark 12:29-31) is that the first commandment is to love God and the second is to love the neighbor as oneself. The two great commandments are ultimately one, for each implies and requires the other. It is the insight recognized by Augustine in the fifth century when he said "Love God and do what you will."

But I am moved to inquire further as to what opens the door to this love which is the great commandment. An answer appears in the Gospel passages about children. In Luke, as well as in Matthew and Mark, Jesus praises children – "'to such belongs the kingdom of God. Truly, I say to you, whoever does not receive the kingdom of God like a child shall not enter it'" (Luke 18:16-17).

And then, like the child's endless Why?, the next question comes rolling out – what does it mean to "receive the kingdom of God like a child"? Did Jesus mean obedience, the answer much stressed by followers of Jesus living in highly authoritarian structures? I do not think that is what Jesus meant. If he did, he could have found a more apt example of obedience than children!

Recalling the early years of my own children and even a few earliest glimpses of my own childhood, I suspect that Jesus was pointing at the openness and spontaneity of children. Love surely embodies taking other people and other things where they are, giving them respect simply for existing as real objects worthy of being loved and cherished by God and by each of us. It is, at bottom, a matter of being in union with the other in such a way that the separateness of each is not completely lost, but is fused into one reality containing both the original parts, the lover and the beloved, each being both lover and beloved.

The openness of children and their ability to find all things new and appreciate them for what they truly are is not itself love, not itself the kingdom. It is, however, the necessary prerequisite for seeing the kingdom around one. It is a childhood talent, one often lost as we become adults and learn how we are supposed to act, a catalog of repression for all seasons. Still, openness and spontaneity were born into us and we can hope to recapture them, however much we have loaded our minds and our behavior with the customs of our place and time. I entertain doubts about the validity of any notion of an "inner child" within myself still seeking care and validation, but only because I am not able to draw so clear a distinction between myself now and the unfulfilled remnant of myself then. I have no doubt that there is a childlike approach to life that is not childish at all and that remains as an ideal behavior for the oldest adult. Openness is all.

To receive the kingdom of God like a child is to be open to love. Love itself is to be open and ever seeking to deepen into the possibilities we encounter every day – that "dearest freshness deep down things" that comes to life for each of us whenever we let down our guard and let it be.

4. The Basis

I've lived in south Texas since 1980. The King Ranch is still a big deal down here. About a million acres, spread over several south Texas counties, it is almost a state within a state. But the great days of the *padrones* – the powerful landowners and politicians – is mostly a memory. George Parr was called the "Duke of Duval County," a place about midway between San Antonio, the Rio Grande and the Gulf of Mexico. A local newspaper reporter, working for the *Corpus Christi Caller-Times* once wrote on the consequences of opposing Boss Parr: "A word from him was sufficient to get a man fired from his job or denied welfare payments or surplus commodities distributed to the needy. Merchants who opposed him faced the sudden loss of most of their trade. Little farmers and ranchers were intimidated by the *pistoleros*."

John Dominic Crossan, in *The Historical Jesus: The Life of a Mediterranean Jewish Peasant*, calls the Roman Empire a "brokered" empire, meaning that the social and economic structure was one centered on patronage. During my years lived in south Texas, I have smelled a faint whiff of what that first century Mediterranean world must have been like. Part of the Spanish dominions in the New

World for centuries, south Texas saw the patron system as a working reality. Life centered around the great haciendas, and later the ranches that occupied the same land. There, the life of the common people was dominated by the *padrone* ruling the estate.

I remember doing some legal work on the sale of a south Texas ranch in which the list of items being transferred contained a reference to the "wetback's house" (finally changed at my insistence). Whether illegal immigrant dependent on the employer for food and protection from the legal authorities, or legal cowboy or ranch hand, one's status, and often one's very ability to live, depended to a large extent on the status and power of the *padrone* with whom one was affiliated.

It all reminded me of earlier experiences in Chicago. Kathleen and I were married there in the days when Richard Daley was in power. When we went down to the Chicago City Hall to get our marriage license in 1970, the marble halls were crowded with overweight, middle and upper aged men, smoking cigars and wearing cheap suits, sitting on benches or walking slowly about with vacant stares – the "clients" of Mayor Daley's patronage machine. Nothing much happened in Chicago without the approval of "Hizzonor duh Mayor."

It wasn't all bad. Occasionally, local responsibility was rewarded. When the residents of Woodlawn, a black and poor section, tired of having their garbage collected once a week, while the rest of the city had service twice a week, they loaded up a garbage truck and dumped the contents at City Hall Plaza. Suddenly the city found time to come by several times a week. They got a similar result – this time a city swimming pool – when they took their own children in cars and buses to swim in the pool provided for the Irish neighborhood where Daley lived.

Whether big city politics or cattle country rule, the systems in Texas and Chicago were more similar than not. Patronage was the name of the game – you didn't get anything, weren't anybody, unless you had a patron. So-

ciety was organized into the dependent masses, the lieu-
tenants/aldermen, and the bosses.

Life around the Mediterranean in the first century
was a lot like that in parts of the American South and
nearly all of the large Northern and Midwestern cities.
Except that the patronage system in the first century was
very probably even more widespread and complete than
its modern counterparts. The whole empire, in Crossan's
phrase, was "brokered." I once labored through a course
in Latin poetry; one of the few things I recall are the
"clients" standing near the doorway of their patron's
house. The first century patronage system embraced all
parts of society, running from the emperor at the top
down to small merchants and rural workers. The patron's
wealth and power was manifested in the number of persons who looked to him for their status. The clients, in
turn, had a known place in society and received support
and favor from the patron. To be outside the patronage
system was to be a nobody, without a recognized position
or life in the world of that time. Every person and every
transaction was brokered by somebody higher up the social food chain

Yet Jesus enters this world and instead of "going
along to get along" (Sam Rayburn – another great master
of political patronage), he refuses to enter into a patronage alliance with anyone or even to attempt setting up
his own patronage system. He eats and drinks with sinners
and drunkards. He cures the outcasts. He takes up as
followers those without any special status. He moves about
the countryside, failing to establish a base of operations.
He goes to the needy, not waiting for them to come and
seek him. He serves at table, even washing the feet of his
followers. A lowly laborer from a tiny village, without status
or power, wealth or connection, he speaks with authority,
yet breaks all the rules that established society used to
judge who had authority, who not.

What did Jesus see that prompted him to act in a
way so contrary to the established order? The answer that

comes to me in the pages of Scripture is not that he saw himself as divine and thus the ultimate broker. Instead, he sees himself as one in relation to God and sees all others whom he encounters as having that same status. The only patron that counts is God and the only real power and status one has is as a child of God.

In his work Jesus deals with all comers, those without status as well as those with status. Moreover, Jesus treats his hearers as having the same status he sees in himself. When the crowd said to him "'your mother and your brothers are outside, asking for you,'" Jesus replied, "'Who are my mother and my brothers?'" Looking at those sitting around him, he says, "'Here are my mother and my brothers! Whoever does the will of God is my brother, and sister, and mother'" (Mark 3:32-35). Astonishingly, he deals with them all as sharing in the same power he has – a power that comes from their true status as sons and daughters of God. All men and women, therefore, are his relatives. He and they are members of the family of God.

Jesus does not set himself up as the mediator, broker or patron of access to God the Father, Instead he instructs his followers to pray to *Our* Father. It is only in the gospel of John, the latest of the collections of Jesus' sayings and actions, that emphasis is placed on Jesus as mediator and the instruction is given to pray to the Father in the name of Jesus. The earlier reports, those of Matthew, Mark and Luke, the ones that consistently show Jesus' actions in contrast with the expectations of his world, place the emphasis on the strength and power of those who love God and neighbor. In so doing, they are in direct contact with God and do not require any patron or broker to succeed.

The basis, for Jesus' message about the present nature of the kingdom, its universal extent and its availability to all open to relationship to God and others in love, is that all human beings are children of God. In Jesus' own life, this relationship, potential in the beginning and needing to be realized in order to come into full actuality, came finally to maturity with Jesus' realization of his own status as a son of God. As teacher, he brings this message to all who listen. They need only become as children, opening themselves to the reality that already surrounds them, to realize that they, too, are children of God, living in the midst of the family of God.

I find God in Jesus, but I find God in the rest of creation as well. The Hindu custom of bowing to others, meaning that the God in one salutes the God in the other, is a custom true to my experience. I think it is the same experience that Jesus found in his own life and that he let shine in his work.

The Life and the Message

For many years I lived from action to action, plunging up or down depending on the response of others. It did not matter much what I thought of what I was doing; I had no center of assurance that allowed me both to assume that I was performing decently and also to allow for the real possibility of error. "Often wrong but never in doubt," people said of me. But that was the outer face, crafted over time to protect the inner void. I judged myself to be whatever response my last action generated.

With time, understanding from my wife and children and some helpful counseling, I began to recover a sense of permanent value. I have become calmer, though far yet from a truly active repose. And the old tapes occasionally replay on the recorder of my soul. A look or a word or an action by another can suddenly trigger the ancient responses. But I sense a new life rising out of richer soil. It looks like a sturdy perennial, not a flashy annual ready to die in the first breeze of autumn. I see it now as a matter of direction of the whole life, not a perpetual judgment of each action. It's not perfect, but even 51% in the right direction and only 49% in the wrong is looking better and better. My life as a whole has taken over from my particular actions. Most of the time, anyway.

There is a cloud of obscurity hovering over all the details of Jesus' life. We can surmise all we want, and research all we can, but there remains always some doubt as to exactly what words Jesus used and what deeds he actually performed. There is no way of completely erasing the possibility that the words were put into his mouth by his followers or those who came along later. The only thing that does seem quite certain is that there was a man, Jesus, who lived in Palestine during the Roman occupation in what is now known as the first century of the Christian era. So, what we have is a definite forest, full of indeterminate trees.

It is, therefore, to the life of Jesus as a whole that we should look for understanding, avoiding special reliance on any particular saying or act. I think of looking at great works of art or hearing a wonderful piece of music. Get too close and the pattern disappears. It is not possible to determine the meaning or the place within the whole of any particular item once it is isolated from its surroundings. A bit of color, a grain of marble, a bark of noise is all we have. Stand back a little, open one's ears to the whole composition and suddenly there is a meaningful totality. It is not just the sum of the individual parts; the work as a whole is a composition that transcends its parts.

In the case of Jesus, the whole life, including his death, points to the message he declared better than any particular piece of that life or death does. The actions of Jesus as he moved about Palestine during the several years between his first appearance to his death are, taken as a whole, a living enactment of the commandment of love, encapsulating the whole of his message on how we should treat one another. The Sermon on the Mount (Matthew 5-7), itself an enlargement of the meaning of the commandment of love, is like a road map of Jesus' life. For what else is it that he does except hunger, mourn, be merciful and be pure in heart. He spends his life coming to the aid of those about him, providing food, seeing into their hearts, curing their ills, and showing them all by his every action what it is to be a child of God.

His death is the final step on the path of his life. His thinking is revolutionary, challenging the political, economic and religious establishment every step of the way. What else could happen other than that he be put to death, stomped out as a nuisance to the authorities and a challenge to their power. He has no power as it was recognized in his own time. All the force is on the side of the establishment, and the establishment uses its power to get rid of this Jesus from Nazareth who teaches by word and action a way of life and an understanding of the world so radically different.

But the death is not an isolated act that in itself saves us. It is simply the final step on the path that Jesus understood himself called to follow. The record suggests that he would have preferred to live rather than undergo crucifixion. But he saw himself as one with an obligation to follow his path to the very end. It would have been a betrayal of his own individual self and the destruction of his own union with God to have turned aside from death, for to do so would have required his compromising his message. He would have to become as the Scribes and Pharisees and deny all that he had spent his life to give to the people.

I am puzzled by the speed with which the Christian community moved away from the picture of Jesus that emerges in the gospels of Matthew, Mark and Luke. How do we move so quickly from a message of the inherent worth of every child of God and the ability of each person to relate directly to God without broker or patron? Instead of a message of enlightenment and self realization, we turn with some rapidity to a message of salvation and redemption brought about by the death of Jesus. Jesus, who did not in his life act as a broker, is made the biggest broker of all time! The message of his life is obscured, although never completely lost in the centuries that follow.

Perhaps I should not be puzzled. My own experience demands of me that I try to understand the message of Jesus in relation to not only my experience of faith in God but also in terms of the world in which I now live. Jesus' first and 10th and 14th-century followers could not escape following the same path. Steeped in religious thinking that traced sin back to the original ancestors, Adam and Eve, and modes of action that always called for a broker, the followers could scarce escape looking for an act affecting all, an act that would counter the original fall, an act performed by an ultimate patron and broker.

Class distinctions and ideas of honor required satisfaction of any offense by someone equal in status to the one offended. God was offended, so only one equal to God can make amends. Forget that a God who would require his own son to be crucified in order that honor be satisfied sounds more like those primitive deities demanding a steady flow of human sacrifice than the God experienced in faith by individuals now. This was the way of thinking prevalent in past times, when it was "obvious" that a human could not propitiate an angry God.

When the student is ready, the teacher appears. It is no accident that Jesus appeared in the west and Prince Siddhartha, the Buddha, appeared in the east within a few hundred years of each other. Human beings were ready for a message of union with God – but perhaps not entirely ready. An understanding of the continuing evolution of all creation and a grasp of the inescapable uncertainty at the heart of matter has prepared us for the message of Jesus better than the science and philosophy of his own time.

Add to that the spread of political democracy. With all its messiness – the trains can be made to run on time, but human beings rarely do – democracy comes out of a sense of individual value. If I think I am nothing, then I must have a patron in order to be anything at all. But if

I am open to an inner conviction of my own value, then I am in a state of readiness to hear Jesus' message about that value and its source in the God who is present within me in an eternal union. Our science and our politics conspire together, not to create a perfect world, but to open us to the continuing possibilities of God and creation.

The traditional theory of atonement, that the divine and human Jesus balanced the scales thrown out of whack by the original sin of Adam and thus saved us from our lost state, fit very well with the scientific and social views of the first century and those of succeeding centuries. They fit, in fact, every time in which status is based on class and fixed categories rather than on possibility and intrinsic worth. The theory of redemption, that Jesus by his death paid the devil's price, buying us back from the evil one, also fits very well in every society where human beings are a commodity rather than individual persons without a commercial price on their heads.

With all the problems that our own time has, I think I see now the possibility that we are in a better place to receive the original message of Jesus than preceding generations were. Political democracy exposes us to the notion of individual worth, as does the opportunity for economic independence. Modern communications and travel and the consequent increase in direct contact with "foreigners" make it more difficult to dismiss all those who are not just like ourselves. It is no accident that Eastern religions emphasizing enlightenment have become attractive to so many, despite the problem raised by the Eastern conception of a heaven or Nirvana where all individuality ultimately disappears. It is enlightenment we need, not salvation.

Jesus' life and death symbolize his message. In fact, they are the message. And the message is that, if you want to follow the teaching of Jesus and come to know your true self as a relative of God, you had best get cracking down your own path of love for God and love for neighbor and self. So, stand up, open out, and breathe in the fresh air!

Jesus and a Divine Nature

Several years ago I read a collection of Joseph Campbell's statements about his life and work, made during various interviews and conferences (*The Hero's Journey: Joseph Campbell on his Life and Work,* edited by Phil Cousineau). At one point Campbell tells about a young nun in his audience who came up to him after one of his talks and asked him whether he believed that Jesus was the Son of God. Campbell's answer was "Not unless all of us are." I felt it as a revelation the first time that I read it. That impact has grown, as with time and effort I have worked at pulling together all the different pieces of my experience as a human being familiar with the Christian tradition. It is, nonetheless, a shocking idea in the light of a tradition that has placed so much emphasis on the singular divinity of Jesus, seeing him as one on an utterly different level of being and existence than those of us who have been thought as sharers solely in his human nature.

In his brief study, *Jesus: A Revolutionary Biography,* John Dominic Crossan says there is nothing surprising about Jesus' followers claiming Jesus was *divine.* There were many claims for divinity in the culture of the time, including the Roman emperors, and small chance for long-lasting attention without an assertion of this sort. What is truly surprising and the really interesting question about Jesus, Crossan argues, is why the followers thought *Jesus* was divine.

However interesting the question of why, there is no doubt that during the first several centuries following Jesus' death, the Christian community formed a belief that Jesus was divine. This conclusion does not appear to be a claim that Jesus made for himself, nor does it appear to be one made by the earliest accounts of his life and sayings, although there is ample evidence that Jesus was seen as extraordinary, with a special relationship with God.

The precise formulation of the later Christian belief, stated by the Council of Chalcedon in the year 451 more than 400 years after Jesus' death, and eventually accepted by most of the Christian communities, was that in Jesus there is one complete and indivisible person but two natures, one divine and one human. Like other official statements of the community's belief made in earlier church councils, it is likely that the intent at Chalcedon was to put some limits on the continuing speculation regarding Jesus' exact status as human, divine or some combination of the two. The subtleties of the original circumstances under which the Chalcedonian formula was made have long since passed into oblivion except in the minds of dedicated scholars. In the popular conception, it looks as if the Monophysites, the group that believed there was only one nature in Jesus, the divine nature, has triumphed. How else explain the glorification of the messenger to the detriment of the message?

The stories and sayings in the first three gospels consistently present a man who is extraordinary but not equivalent to God. The last gospel, that of John, and later tradition move in the direction of a unique, qualitative difference between Jesus and all other human beings. He is the Word, the second person of the triune God. What can I, living 2,000 years after Jesus, make of this disparity? I cannot, certainly, leave the subject of my understanding of Jesus without looking at how best to deal with historic belief in Jesus as divine while still remaining faithful to my faith experience. How am I to take into account all of my modern experience while still expressing my faith in a statement of belief that is connected to my Christian tradition?

I am convinced from both my own experience and from reading the gospel accounts of Jesus life, particularly those of Matthew, Mark and Luke, as well as the *Gospel of*

Thomas (one of the several early collections about Jesus that did not get into the official New Testament collection), that Jesus' message placed his hearers on the same level as himself, so that if we are to conclude that Jesus is more than a human being totally separated from God, we must at the same time conclude that we also are more than simply separated human beings. Perhaps the best way to say this is to say that Jesus and we, too, are children of God – not God in the sense of the ground and source of all that exists, but children of God in that we share in a limited way in the divinity that has spread itself out in the world through its ongoing and self actualizing creativity.

It is the only view available that makes any sense at all of Jesus' teachings about the here and now quality of the kingdom, its presence everywhere for everyone, and its accessibility to all those who will, like children, look around them with open and loving eyes. Jesus, somehow, some way during those first 30 years of his life, came to realize that he, while remaining fully human, was also in immediate union with God. He came to a shattering moment of self realization and then moved outward to spread this good news to all who would be open to look and see. As teacher, not as patron or mediator or broker, he tells us about our own condition and state and how we and he are bound together in one great community of persons in union with God and with each other. That is already our condition from birth, just as it was his. What is new, first for him and then for us, is our own realization of that condition. In that realization we come to share in the fullness of humanity Jesus has. We share with him a realization of union with God and union with all of creation.

The tradition of the unique divinity of Jesus has always contained within itself its own seeds of contradiction. Christian tradition has moved back and forth on the question whether salvation is obtained through performing good works or by faith alone. Hold strongly to the divinity of Jesus and the fallen nature of human beings and the logical answer appears to be that we are saved, if at all, by faith in Jesus. But, if that is so, what is the point of performing good works – feeding the hungry and all the things that Jesus asked. If we really have to do them, then faith is not enough. Formulas are devised to hide the problem – "faith clothed in good works," – but the problem is stubborn and will not be buried.

Then there's codependency, which is looking more and more like the occupational disease of traditional Christianity. I think of the many Christians I've encountered who base their religious lives on following the rules handed them on an ecclesiastical platter. These Christians have no independent reality. Their actions seem no more than a response to the acts of another. "I" and "we" disappear and there remains only what "the Lord has told me or us to do." The result is either a person or group so devoid of individuality that the very reason for existence has been lost. Or, on occasion, there is a rampant but unacknowledged individuality where action proceeds in total selfishness while clothing itself in Jesus' garments.

I've had many experiences with those who insisted they were only following the commands of Jesus. I can't recall any that were good. When I hear "this hurts me more than it hurts you," I'm pretty certain there's going to be a lot of doodoo on my floor!

When we go all the way back to Jesus, we get the full and shocking good news. We are closest to God when we are most fully ourselves. The conflict between faith and works, the barrier between God and human beings, collapses into a union of diverse individuals. This is not either/or but both/and, a world where faith and works are only different sides of the same mountain, and where God and human beings coexist, each in fulfillment of the needs of the other.

Those who followed after Jesus and the earliest communities of his followers, were not, understandably enough, always able to withstand the shock of realization.

Little by little, the Tradition drifted into an either/or attitude about God and creation. There was God on the one side and fallen creation on the other, each totally distinct from the other. According to this way of thinking, a mediator was required in order for fallen creation to come back into a relationship with God. Jesus came to be seen as fulfilling this mediator's role. By turning Jesus into the one being combining within himself both the essence of God and the essence of creation, the Tradition found a way to bridge a gap it had come to believe was otherwise unbridgeable. Everyone needs a patron and a mediator and Jesus became that patron and mediator.

The message of self realization or enlightenment is turned into a message of salvation. The efficacy of salvation is assured by the divinity of Jesus. The insistence on the divine quality of the messenger, which might have been a way of pointing to the significance of the message, turns into a cloud that first obscures and then finally hides the message itself. The final state is that of popular belief 1,900 years after the event. The miracles and virgin birth, resurrection and ascension are taken as literal descriptions of actual events instead of mythological ways of putting emphasis on the importance of the original message of enlightenment and self realization. And the shocking good news – that we are all children of God in a very literal sense – becomes a pale metaphor, devoid of its original impact. We have turned the message of Jesus upside down in order to preserve cultural traditions.

* * * * *

Those religious believers within the tradition of the East have to deal with the occupational disease of letting creation and God collapse into identity. Those religious believers within the tradition of the West have to deal with the occupational disease of allowing the unity of God and creation to explode and separate into two utterly distinct stars, held together if at all only by the gravity of Jesus.

The reality is that God and creation exist together in a union that is always indissoluble, although not always recognized. Jesus recognized it and taught us about it.

It is not a message or a balance that can be developed in a series of logical steps. The third-century Christian writer, Tertullian, was right when he said, "I believe because it is absurd." The union of God and creation is absurd as a logical proposition, because logic can only deal with separate and discrete things. It is reachable in faith, however, because faith deals with forests, not just with individual trees. It experiences the whole, while not losing the parts.

Jesus teaches enlightenment, he does not deliver salvation. Or, it may be that it is more correct to say that enlightenment is salvation. It is this very enlightenment that gives us the courage to consciously love God and all creation around us, to grow into whatever the future holds and by our willingness to open ourselves to growth, to make that future a continuing possibility.

I once heard an elderly Catholic priest asked to join with a group of other priests to "concelebrate" the Mass, a then new way of having a community celebration rather than having Masses performed by individual priests. No fan of the new ways, he yelled back, "No, I don't want to be a spear carrier in a mob scene!" I think he misunderstood what concelebration was all about, but it was easy to sympathize with his intuition that individuality should not be submerged and lost, as it has been so often in communities of believers where we are only a mob dependent on Jesus for all of our reality. That is not what he told us that we are.

So, in response to the question whether Jesus is the Son of God, the only answer I can give is Yes, but so are we all.

CHAPTER SEVEN

The Faithful Community

The genius of Christianity is to have proclaimed that the path to the deepest mystery is the path of love.
— Andre Malraux, *Anti-Memoirs*

It takes a great deal of Christianity to wipe out uncivilized Eastern instincts, such as falling in love at first sight.
— Rudyard Kipling, *Plain Tales from the Hills*

"The Christian ideal," it is said, "has not been tried and found wanting; it has been found difficult and left untried."
— G. K. Chesterton, *What's Wrong with the World*

Makes them feel more important to be prayed over in Latin.
— James Joyce, *Ulysses*

We visit Notre Dame cathedral in Paris late one Sunday morning in July. Warm outside, it is cool but not dark within. A priest is offering Mass at the altar located under the great arches where the nave, choir and transepts meet. A crowd of believers fills the central aisle; other visitors walk in the outer aisles, mostly oblivious to what occurs at the center. So many people, they say, that

*the moisture of their breath has begun to affect the glass filling
the walls, soaring above the floor.*

*Medieval builders discovered a way to bring light into their
churches. Long before steel structures, curtain walls of glass freed
churches from the thick walls once needed to support the roof.
Flying buttresses, located outside the cathedral, carried part of
the weight outward and then down, reducing the space needed
for pillars within. After raising the main pillars, the builders
constructed a light wooden scaffolding. Upon this platform they
installed first the arching ribs of stone connecting pillar to pillar
in a network of stone lines. Then they filled the spaces between
the ribs with stone vaulting, all finally capped by a few inches
of lightweight concrete. When the vaults were completed, the
wooden scaffolding was removed. If all had been done well and
the materials were solid, it continued to stand. It was all a matter
of fine balance. The flying buttresses pressed inwards, countering
the load of the arched stone vaults, in turn supporting the weight
of the lead covered roof. All had to be built together, joined in
unison, so that no force was ever unbalanced by lack of a counter
force.*

*From the middle of the twelfth century to the middle of the
thirteenth century a cathedral building explosion took place,
towns competing with one another to raise ever larger and loftier
churches, for the glory of God, the self esteem of the city dwellers,
and the enrichment of merchants profiting from the surge of
pilgrims. We marvel (or shudder) at the competition among our
cities to build sports palaces. What would we think if every city
of 40,000 or more built a stadium large enough to hold all its
inhabitants? In medieval France, cities of only 10- or 15,000
inhabitants were raising cathedrals large enough for everyone in
the town to attend a single Mass.*

*And what cathedrals! Spacious and light, and always
higher and higher, as if to touch and enclose God within the
arching stones. The vaults at Notre Dame in Paris (1163) soar
107.6 feet above the floor. Chartres (1194) reaches 119.9 feet;
Rheims (1212) 124.5 feet and Amiens (1221) 138.8 feet. Beauvais (1228), loftiest of all, soared to 157.5 feet. But, at Beauvais,
the nave collapsed in 1284. A fissure in a stone or two, a design*

*fault, poor workmanship, a reach of imagination beyond its grasp
– who knows?*

*Notre Dame in Paris has stood for eight centuries. But it
requires constant attention. A small crack, widened a little by
freezing rain or snow, stone eroded by air pollution, it would
not take much neglect for things to fall apart. Ozymandias lurks
in the shadows.*

Finding Favor Among the People

Several years ago Kathleen and I were increasingly dis-
tressed by the lack of a community of faithful believers.
We were regularly attending a church, a Roman Catholic
one, but we went more from a vague compulsion to belong
to something than from any deep conviction that the
community embodied an expression of a heartfelt experience of faith. The words of an aunt came to mind. She
sometimes had a job, sometimes did not. When out of
work, her standard reply to questions about what she was
doing was that she was "between positions." We were, I
thought, between communities. Our old one was fading
into nonexistence. A new one had not yet appeared.

We did not know what it was that we hoped to find.
But we must have been keeping our ears open, enough
at least to hear of a a recently formed group. It was meeting
only a few blocks from where we lived, but we heard about
it while attending a conference for business and professional people concerned about religion held several hundred miles from Corpus Christi. Listening to our
expressions of desire for a community that did more than
merely gather once a week for a standard service and
sermon, someone asked us if we were aware of a new
Episcopal church in our city. By this time both of us were
desperate enough not to shy away from anything outside
our own church of birth, so we visited that new church
the first Sunday after our return.

I don't recall what we expected to find. The regular priest was away for the weekend. The service – morning prayer – was led by a member of the congregation. Everyone apologized that we did not have the chance to meet the pastor. But no need for apologies. Somehow we were made to feel greatly welcome. There was conversation before and after the service, and the service itself was at once simple and moving. Out of the Book of Common Prayer, it was carried out in a way that came alive. Not a repetition of something grown long familiar and repeated out of unattending memory, the words seemed fresh, not just to us hearing them for the first time but obviously to all those there. And the little talk given by the service leader was not about rules and duties or a distant God or sins, but about practical ways and means of reaching out to help those outside the group. Food for the hungry, a place to sleep for the unhoused, help in finding a job for someone unemployed.

The memory of our excitement is still strong. As it developed, flies appeared in this paradise. But for a brief moment this small church had a strong touch of what it was we were seeking. More conscious now of the search and the signs than I was then, I am better able to bring to the surface of mind what it was that attracted me in the first experience of that small church community fanning itself into flame.

*   *   *   *   *

In 1966, when I was studying theology at the Jesuit house of studies in Woodstock, Maryland and awaiting ordination as a Roman Catholic priest, I wrote an article about what it meant to be a member of a church and what had occurred at the original Pentecost. I reread that article recently and discovered that one of life's more pleasant surprises is to find some genuine continuity in one's experiences and ideas. In the midst of all this change, there really is an enduring thread. Or maybe it's just the truth of the old French saying that "the more things change, the more they remain the same."

The article was a reflection on my experience of belonging to a church, a community of faithful believers. The purpose of the article was to draw a picture of what it meant to belong to such a community. The message of the article was that there was a double way in which such a community existed. First, it existed as an experience, the church community as it was summed up in the description of the first Christians found in Acts 2:44-47: "And all who believed were together and had all things in common; and they sold their possessions and goods and distributed them to all, as any had need. And day by day, attending the temple together and breaking bread in their homes, they partook of food with glad and generous hearts, praising God and having favor with all the people."

The first and deepest experience of the church community was of being part of a group, living together, praying together, eating together. And not just a private group, but one that was seen by the public as a place of peace and love and generosity – for why else would the group have "found favor" with all the people? If anything is clear in the Scriptural account, it is that the appeal to others was in the life led by the members of the community, rather than in some doctrine that they may have taught.

The second meaning of the church community, I had written, was found in its self understanding – the Pentecost event, when the spirit of God entered into the minds and hearts of the disheartened and mourning followers of the dead Jesus. In union with God, the followers came to understand their own lives and situation. They were finally able to grasp what it was that Jesus had tried to tell them by his own life and death.

The center of the teaching of Jesus and of the life of the first communities of faithful believers is that the heart of the faithful community is found in the actions of that community. As in the gospel story of Jesus' appear-

ance to the two followers walking along the road to Emmaus after Jesus' death, Jesus (and union with God) is
found in such humdrum actions as eating a meal together.
Meeting a stranger along the Emmaus road, the travelers
invite him to stay with them for the evening meal. "When
he was at table with them, he took the bread and blessed,
and broke it, and gave it to them. And their eyes were
opened and they recognized him; and he vanished out of
their sight" (Luke 24:30-31). God does not unite with us
in the abstract. God is found in those ordinary events of
our daily lives where we open ourselves to others by sharing what we have.

The earliest experience of the church, the community of Christian faithful, was recognized by those surrounding the community. It is not difficult to hear, even
now, the whisper of those seeing that community: "See
how those Christians love one another." Neither is it difficult to understand how the sight attracted and supplied
a flow growing to a flood of new members. Being a community of love and sharing is the first and most fundamental mark of any group claiming to be followers of
Jesus.

The earliest times of shared, loving community
passed quickly. Turn to the scriptural account found in
Revelation, and the tone is not just 50 or 60 years distant,
but a world apart. The writer, in his comments about the
churches of Asia Minor, sounds the tones of a nagging
modern pastor. The emphasis is all on what is being done
wrong – sacrificing to idols, eating forbidden foods, har-
boring sinners within the community! What Jesus would
have understood and dealt with in love and openness is
now cause for condemnation. The lines were drawn once
again between "us" and "them."

The long history of the Christian churches has been
more a history of oppression, religious wars, condemnations, judgments, hatreds and strife than of openness,
love, understanding and recognition of the union with
God that is at the heart of all human beings. Small wonder

that a 20th-century Zen Buddhist philosopher could say of Christianity: "Nature against God. God against nature. Nature against man. Man against nature. Man against God. God against man. Very funny religion" (Daisetz Suzuki, quoted in *The Hero's Journey: Joseph Campbell on His Life and Work*, edited by Phil Cousineau).

Looking for a Community

As the months passed, Kathleen and I kept running up against problems in the new Corpus Christi church we had joined with much enthusiasm. It never got to the parking lot demolition derby feeling of our previous Catholic Church experience, where the parishioners seemed locked in a demented competition to get out of the church, into their cars and home as quickly as possible. But there were subtle pressures that infiltrated the spirit of openness that had been the early attraction. As one member put it to me months later when I ran into him at the supermarket checkout line, there was an inner circle and you had better do it their way if you wanted full acceptance.

Tithing was a particular stumbling block for me. A basis in Scripture it might have, but with two children in college, a third about to start, a mortgage and some heavy uncertainties about my work, I didn't see giving 10% of income to the church as a real possibility. More than that, even if the amount had not been a problem, I felt an instinctive resistance to the idea that this ancient practice was still as applicable as it might have been in a time when the church was the primary source of help to those in material need. But there it was. By this time I was a member of the vestry – the members of the congregation that, along with the priest, determined local policy matters – expected to lead the way in giving. I felt pressured to do something whose rationale I felt no longer existed and was, in any event, hardly possible to meet.

A second area of disturbance was the church's growth and building program. The addition of new members required, it seemed, additional space. The additional space would require further new members in order to fund payment. Further growth would require even more space. And so on in a relentless upward spiral that some believed was the true sign that the church was complying with God's will. Church growth looked more and more like the criterion for success, not the spirit of open acceptance and concern for others that had originally brought us into the community.

Reflecting on joining a church that now bore so many similarities to the one I had left, I thought of Dr. Johnson's characterization of remarriage following divorce – the "triumph of hope over experience." Finally, I resigned from the vestry and left the community. There was a considerable amount of sadness but also a sense of relief that the oppressive burden of carrying a church was gone. The entire experience had one good and lasting effect – it caused me to look more carefully and thoroughly at just what it was I sought. What was I looking for in a community of faithful believers?

The "marks" of the church that I was taught many years ago are "one, holy, catholic and apostolic." I don't find them very helpful in either describing or identifying religious communities that are alive and well. There may be nothing really wrong with these traditional marks. But they sound too much like characteristics heard from the outside, as if finding a religious community were like shopping for a car. *Consumer Reports* in hand, you go from showroom to showroom, inquiring about horsepower, height, width and length, safety devices, mileage, checking each item off until you find the one car with the most approved qualities. You can look for a church the same way, I suppose, if you think of it as a commodity.

I am moved to believe, instead, that there are some inner marks which are less observable by an outsider than the official marks. They have to be experienced within rather than viewed from without.

1. Helping Hands

"Home," Robert Frost wrote, "is the place where, when you have to go there, They have to take you in" ("The Death of the Hired Man"). That's not bad – better to have one place where they have to take you in than none at all! But I want and expect my church, the community of faithful believers, to do a little better than that. That community should be the place where, when you go there, they *want* to take you in. Its treatment of both its own members and outsiders should rise out of a recognition of the common humanity and the common union with God in each person rather than out of a sense of ecclesiastical obligation.

That desire to take you in, if founded in a recognition of God within us all, will demonstrate itself in the helping hands of the community. Whether it is providing shelter for the homeless, feeding the hungry, finding work for the unemployed or simply listening to the guest's story, the community's work will be to bring aid appropriate to the state and condition of the one at its doorstep. The old Benedictine motto was "A guest comes, Christ comes." As someone once said to me, that attitude has often been perverted by Christian communities into "A guest comes, Christ comes – crucify him!" But the feeling and idea of seeing Jesus in each guest is fully in line with the gospel's teaching that what we do to those around us is done to Christ. It is also fully in harmony with a faith experience of the union with God of all beings. What the Benedictine motto underlines is that a piece of God is in every one, and that calls for recognition and special treatment.

So the quality of helping hands, with openness and joy in the face of all comers, is the first mark, for me, of any community that claims to be a community of faithful believers.

2. *Attentive Ears*

Cardinal Manning, a Roman Catholic clergyman in Victoria's England, is supposed to have said that the role of the nonclergy members of the church was to pray, to pay and to obey. Like good Victorian children, the people in the pews were expected to be seen but not heard. In my experience, little has changed in most churches today. In the midst of all the noise of doctrine and judgment, few are allowed to speak, hardly anyone is heard. Hearing, if it exists at all, is reduced to a hearing of the word of God as filtered through the mouths of the clergy.

Several months ago I was in Chicago visiting a sister-in-law who is an administrator and faculty member at Loyola University. On Sunday we went to Mass at the university chapel. Recently renovated, with a splendid new plaza in front facing Lake Michigan, the church, more than many an imitation of Gothic or Romanesque cathedral, seemed conducive to a gathering of the community. Instead of the streetcar arrangement of pews facing forwards towards a distant altar, chairs had been placed in a shallow semicircle, facing an altar at one side of the church. A piano and bass fiddle were there to provide music. The community waiting for the priest was mostly middle aged, more women than men, but obviously attentive and expectant. I thought that this might be about as good as it could get in the traditional church.

As the service progressed, however, something kept troubling me. It finally hit me that here, with this highly educated audience of university students and professors, there was no sharing at all. The listening and hearing was all one way. The priest had a message and he delivered it reasonably well. But there was no response, no comment, no added insight or experience coming from the rest of the community. Didn't any of the people have anything at all to say? What had they been doing all their lives? Where were they now? What might they tell the rest of us, if given a chance? Did only the priest have access to the word of God?

In most traditional Christian churches there is no real communication. Faith, they say, comes from hearing. But the traditional hearing is from the top down, with the vast bulk of the community destined forever to listen and forever to respond only by a dull nodding of the head, which may be closer to a drowsy sleep than any of those in authority would want to acknowledge.

Part of the priest's message was to stand up and speak out. But he didn't expect or want anyone there in front of him to stand up and speak out. Any speaking up and standing out on the part of the people facing the priest was to occur in passing on the received message to those outside the fold. I didn't stand up or speak out either, but the experience added fuel to my conviction that I would seek a place where hearing was a two way street. Attentive ears were what I wanted – attentive ears on everyone's heads, not just on the heads of those in the pews. And ears that not only heard but really listened

Having attentive ears doesn't mean letting others speak while thinking how to respond to their "errors." That may be a kind of hearing, but it is not listening. Hearing without listening is easy. It is the customary preliminary to judging, at least among those Christian groups willing to let others say something instead of going immediately to the favored sport of telling everyone outside the group (and most of those within it) how sinful, evil, wrong, erroneous (you fill in the blank) they are.

Having attentive ears means listening for the message behind the expressions. It is getting to what mediators of legal disputes call the "interests" underlying the "positions." I find myself talking, most of the time, in canned language that disguises what I really want to express. I am often locked into saying what I think people expect me to say, and I have come to believe that others often do the same. So, to get at what the person you are listening to is really trying to express, you have to become something of a cryptographer. Break the code and find the hidden inner message. It may be body language or it may be a certain way the actual words spoken are working. There is almost always something behind the words that is deeper than and may even contradict the speaker's words.

Listening during a recent election campaign to those claiming membership in the Christian political right, I sensed something more going on than a desire to return to a mythical Valueland where all children instantly obeyed their teachers and parents (all of whom were patient, learned and loving), crimes were committed only by the irreligious and evil, politicians were incorruptible, Christians were well above average in cleanliness and Godliness, and everyone else made up the statistical balance by being way below average. Getting at the root of what is bothering these people takes considerable patience. What is finally revealed is a lot of pain and fear in the hearts of people faced with a culture that they believe wants to trivialize their concerns and deepest interests. It turns out that we have a lot in common – they, too want to be heard, acknowledged and respected.

Listening with patience finally has a reward – we discover that a human being exists beneath the layers of hateful language and condemnation. Someone is crying out for attention and an opportunity to be heard and be accepted as a human being. If the anger rises within you as you listen to those with whom disagreement seems greatest, then it may be a sign of your own unresolved problems. Listening for the message behind the words of others increases your ability to hear the message behind your own words. If you can't cure all the ills about you, working on your ears will help you cure your own ills!

I, along with everyone I know, want to be heard. But we all need help in saying what we really mean. A community of faithful believers ought to be able to do that for its own members and for those outside its membership. If it can't, it's not a community of faithful believers. It's more likely just a collection of hanging judges.

3. Patient Minds

I remember waiting each spring for the ice to disappear from Lake Michigan and the water to warm just a trifle, so that I could jump in. It was a lot of fun. So is the fresh cold water of new ideas, and the more of them the better!

It was not always so. I recall, not so many years ago wondering whether I would ever find a stable system of thought. Plato was intriguing; Aristotle was immensely attractive. Augustine's thought had its depths in personal experience; the system of Aquinas was a vast compelling architectural network of thought. Calvin and Luther added new pieces; Descartes brought intellectual clarity. And Kant turned it all upside down, like a philosophical Copernican revolution. Who to hold to? Where was the central rock which I could grasp in the conflicting currents stirred by these great thinkers of the past?

I think I have come to a more patient turn of mind. Now it is easier to accept and appreciate what has gone before, without the oppressive need to select one to the detriment of the others. And I have learned not to expect a new synthesis any time soon. In fact, I have begun to suspect that there may never again be a new synthesis. Just an unfolding mystery.

Looking over nearly two millennia of Christian expressions of the faith of the community, there is a noticeable ebb and flow. The earliest times show great uncertainty about the proper way to express the faith of the community. Over the ensuing three or four centuries, this uncertainty gradually moved toward fixed expressions in the statements made by the councils of the church held at Nicea, Ephesus, and Chalcedon. Greek philosophy, particularly the ideas of philosophers tracing their roots back to Plato, provided a framework in which the community of the faithful was able to find satisfying expression. Augustine, writing in the early fifth century, was at the peak of this development.

The decline of the Roman Empire and the following centuries of strife left the Augustinian synthesis of Christian thought largely undisturbed. Not until the early medieval period, with the entry of new scientific knowledge from Arab scholars and the introduction of the line of thought tracing itself to Aristotle rather than to Plato did Christian thought bubble once again. The great medieval synthesis, triumphant in the formulations of Aquinas and his followers, finally emerged, taking the place of the Augustinian synthesis. Scholasticism – the systems of belief taught in the "schools" following the medieval masters – has remained central ever since in the Roman Catholic church's understanding of its faith. If the Protestant churches took different paths in the works of Luther, Calvin and others, it is probably not too much to say that these were reactions to the systems of Aquinas and other medieval theologians rather than genuinely new departures.

But we are now again at a moment of changing tides. The medieval synthesis, still beautiful like the Gothic cathedrals built during the same era, is no longer capable of providing a system of thought for a faithful community that is at the same time immersed in a modern world of scientific discovery and new methods of seeking satisfactory explanations of the world of facts. Even those not themselves scientists cannot avoid the impact of modern science. "If," Daniel J. Boorstin writes, "we cannot grasp the meanings of Einstein's theories of special and general relativity, or the implications of quantum mechanics, we still can have some general impression of how and where modern discoveries are pointing" (*Cleopatra's Nose: Essays on the Unexpected*). Wherever they are pointing, they are not pointing at the medieval synthesis or at the later movements flowing out of or reacting to that synthesis.

In a time of ebb tide, the mind has to be patient, waiting for the strength of the waters to regather and once again approach the flood. That thought should be sufficient to teach us to be patient with all the new ideas calling for acceptance. The cream will rise to the surface, but it will take some time. The Augustinian synthesis and the medieval synthesis were centuries in the making; we cannot hurry the process. So, at the very least, a contemporary community of faithful believers should be prepared to sit back patiently and let all possible cooks take a stab at preparing a new feast.

In this historical moment, repression of new ideas is certain to make the process of forming a new set of central ideas even longer than it would otherwise be. The faithful community will be able to withhold judgment and let new ideas come forth. Time will give them the lie or recognize their validity. When the unexpected is more likely than the expected to shine a clear light on our uncertainties and doubts, the faithful community will honor the unexpected.

But there is the possibility and the promise of more. The ebb and flow of the older systems as well as the particular approach of modern scientists strongly suggests that all syntheses are in time doomed to die. There is ultimate truth in experience but not in sets of ideas attempting to explain that experience. What I find in book after book by contemporary scientists is the notion that all syntheses are simply theories, more or less valid in providing us with a systematic understanding of the ever growing, endless mountain ranges of data. The last great scientific hope, the formulation of GUT, the Grand Unified Theory combining into one synthesis gravity, electromagnetism and the strong and weak nuclear forces, seems on the ropes – not because a formulation is not still possible, but rather because any such formulation is itself likely to be finally found inadequate to the mysteries yet to be uncovered in immensities of space and time pregnant with the unexpected.

In an ultimate exercise of patience, our minds may finally give up the notion of an ultimate intellectual system holding in its confines all the mysteries of the universe. If I am anywhere near right, not even God knows what the final system would be, or even if there can be a final system. Instead of working to establish and defend such a system, we will learn to live with our faith experiences and sets of partial ideas, expecting only the unexpected.

4. Faithful Hearts

I try to recall what it is about those few people I have met who have embodied what has seemed to be a faithful heart. It is not a habit of keeping the rules or of constantly doing what is supposed to be done. Neither is it a blind acceptance of doctrine or a thoughtless following of a leader. What I think I have seen is something of that peace and centredness that I have encountered in myself on a few brief occasions. It is a sense of being united to the heart of the universe, of participating in a glowing fire of existence that enlightens without burning, eternal yet caught in a moment of time.

Not everyone in the community of faithful believers will have this quality of a faithful heart fully, but all will have at least a little of it and an appreciation of it. If it is not yet fully realized, it will be acknowledged as the goal and recognized in others. Without this quality of being centered and whole in the community, there will be no community in any real sense, only a gathering of individuals, each without a center and all together with no center, only a form of external conformity. A faithful heart knows no class or age or sex. It may not exist at all in those whose external qualities would raise expectations of finding inner light. It may exist in those whose education or role in society or age or experience would make it seem unlikely to the logical mind. Finding it is a joyful surprise. You know it when you see it. It is a real moment in real time.

A faithful heart is the summation and the inspiring force of helping hands, attentive ears and patient minds. Together these four qualities are what I look for as the new marks of the church, the things I want and expect to find in a modern faithful community.

Is Anyone In Charge Here?

I've come to have a lot of affection for Father Sorin, the French priest who founded the University of Notre Dame. If he hadn't succeeded, Knute Rockne and the Fighting Irish wouldn't have been around to make autumn Saturday afternoons exciting.

Father Sorin came from France to Indiana with several companions in the middle years of the nineteenth century. He was able to obtain the right to use some land in unsettled areas in the northern part of the state. Traveling there in the winter, he finally managed to establish his school a few miles north of the St. Joseph River. He dedicated it to Notre Dame du Lac, Our Lady of the Lake, failing to realize that there were not one but two lakes hidden under the all covering snows.

Then came the interesting part. He needed to obtain authorization from Rome. Letters went out from Indiana to Rome, letters in due course returned. The requests were made. They were usually denied. But by the time the denial reached Sorin, what he had requested was already in place. So, further letters detailing what had happened, with further requests. Further denials, Rome always six months to a year behind the pace.

Rome, always better at accommodating something already in place than to approve anything new, finally recognized what Sorin had accomplished. Notre Dame survived and grew, not least because of the time it took for communications to run between Rome and Indiana. Along with "Touchdown Jesus" and "First Down Moses," Sorin is memorialized by a statue on the Notre Dame campus, and my son Colin spent four years there in a residence hall named after him. A great example of what a determined individual used to be able to do even in the face of Roman opposition!

Times have changed but not for the better. What used to take months or years now occurs in the seconds it requires for Rome to be informed by telephone or facsimile of what is going on anywhere in the world, and then respond with instant and insistent command. It may be that Gutenberg's invention of the printing press was, as a friend claims, the real source of Rome's troubles at the time of the Protestant Reformation. Modern telecommunications have given Rome an opportunity for revenge. It can now make decisions before anything irreversible has occurred. And the opportunity for an immediate answer feeds the hunger of those who prefer the expected to the unexpected. If it isn't something already approved, Just Say No!

Given the structure of the Roman Empire in the first centuries after Jesus' death, it is not at all surprising that the government of the Christian community would take on the appearance of an imperial hierarchy. Neither is it surprising that the bishops of the medieval period would follow the lead of the local barons in centralizing religious power, and that Rome would follow in transferring much of that power to itself as the centralized nation states of Europe rose. But what is one to make of this colossus of centralized authority in a period of democracy? When the Pope visited Mexico several yeas ago, he encouraged the spread of freedom and more democratic government there. An astonishing position, a friend remarked, to be held by the head of the last authoritarian government in Europe!

Leadership is not likely to be absent from the community of faithful believers. There will always be those who by birth or education will have an influence on those about them. Leaders will arise in the faithful community through a process of recognition and acceptance by the other members of the group. If they understand their role and how they obtained it, these leaders will listen to and respect the experience of all members of the community, and they will be hesitant to give orders and commands, preferring to wait until a true consensus has been reached.

It would not, I think, hurt at all and would probably do a great deal of good in my familiar world of Roman Catholicism if the local community had a voice in what priest would be present to serve them, and in what bishop operated in their area. It doesn't seem inherently contradictory for God to be in union with those who have been elected – surely no more difficult than being in union with those chosen by distant authorities. Pointing to the common custom of giving sitting bishops a say in who their successor would be, and noting that many might have distanced themselves from anyone who might outshine them, the theory arose that a kind of downward spiral had been at work for centuries, explaining what kind of religious authority figures are available now. Cynical, but maybe a bit of truth in it. A good dose of democracy might raise all of our boats!

It is not a matter of taking a vote on what Christianity is all about, as authoritarians claim in attempting to belittle the views of those who do not adore at the altar of absentee authority. Instead, it is a matter of waiting for the community to recognize what its experience, at a given time and place, is saying. Attentive ears and patient minds should be the mark most especially of anyone claiming to speak for the whole group.

In our contemporary community of faithful believers, the job of authority is not to define who has won and who has lost the game. It is to keep the ball in play. Its principal action will be to encourage experiment and discussion. By its actions, it will help us all understand more fully that living a faithful life is a process, not a matter of learning a set of established rules and applying them blindly.

There is one nice little sign of hope. Extremes seem to engender their opposites, and the aggressiveness of Rome in asserting its authority may be another example proving that rule. Unintentionally, Rome has been doing all of us looking for open listening a favor. Burdened by their own conception of duty (to discover and ferret out "error" as quickly as possible), orthodox authority figures are much given to prohibiting discussion rather than taking an open look at the questions. There is nothing more likely to make we Americans, infused with a sense of democracy and challenge, take great interest in an issue than to have it put on the list of prohibited topics. So, I don't look for questions about married clergy and women priests or contraception or abortion to go away simply because someone in Rome or anywhere else says they are beyond discussion. They will continue to be discussed and, in the process, we all learn that continued probing and questioning is good.

There is a Chinese curse: "May you live in interesting times." We don't have much choice about the times in which we live, and these times of ours are decidedly interesting! But I have come to believe that this is not really a curse at all. A strong dose of turmoil challenges us all to act better, think better, be better. Across the Texas border in Louisiana, the Cajuns like to say "Laissez les bonnes temps rouler" – "Let the good times roll." For those in love with God and the universe, it's a pretty good motto for a lot of things. And it suggests a complementary rule for our moment in the history of God and the universe: "Let the interesting times roll!"

Does This Game Have Any Rules?

I have a confession to make. It is time for me to admit that I do not know what "objectively sinful acts" are. The phrase keeps recurring in statements from my church of origin, but I have found it more and more difficult to understand. I think I understand what a sinful act is – a particular act of an individual human being that is destructive of that individual's union with God and the universe. It is the *objectively* sinful act that goes beyond me. I can trace the difficulty at least as far back as my first year studying philosophy in the Jesuits. At the year end exam, when asked which was the more true, the universal (and objective, that is, unaffected by any of the limitations found in all individual subjects) concept of human or a single individual human being, I answered (knowing it was not the "right" answer) that it was the single human being. I still think individuals alone are truly real, and that objective concepts are ideas whose whole reality is only derivative from actual real beings. An objectively sinful act is a concept, and individuals don't commit concepts.

But all rules are concepts. So can the rules have any authority other than what comes from an arbitrary agreement or as passing fads and fancies? We drive on the right; it's the rule of the road. But we know we could change our laws and drive on the left. After all, they do it that way in England, Scotland, Ireland and Japan without noticeable moral harm – and we better do it that way, too, when we are in any of those countries! Are our moral laws or rules any different than the rules of the road? Can they be changed at will or by an accident of history, so that suddenly it is all right to lie, steal, murder or whatever?

The real problem with moral laws and rules is that we have given them a greater claim to universality than they deserve. Derived from the real world of actual individual beings, they do have a limited truth and validity. The limitation is not that they are subject to change at will, but that they are true or adequate only to the extent they fully reflect the situation they are called upon to judge. Since the moral laws are abstract ideas, they are always to some extent inadequate. Because of their abstract quality they do not contain all the parts and pieces of the individual situation, the only place where a moral decision has to (or can) be made.

Take an old issue – whether slavery is morally wrong. Paul, in one of his epistles to the early churches, says that slaves should obey their masters, implicitly condoning the then widespread Roman custom of owning slaves. For centuries the Christian religious communities had no great problem with slavery, protesting it primarily, if at all, when it was a question of non-Christians enslaving Christians. The Maryland Province of the Society of Jesus owned slaves prior to the Civil War, and so did many Christians living in the American South.

The growth of the antislavery movement in the 18th and 19th centuries finally led to a recognition that slavery was morally wrong. How did this happen? The key to the development was the recognition of a humanity common to all, and the further recognition that slavery was a denial of the humanity of the enslaved. The opposing concept of the value of property rights could not finally stand against this new recognition of the full humanity of the slaves. The moral view that slavery was acceptable had to change because of the expanded recognition of what the real situation was.

The same thing happened in the development of the Christian view that there were certain situations in which it was not immoral to kill – the "just war" theory developed by Augustine ended a period of dispute whether it was moral or immoral for Christians to be members of the Roman army, fight battles and kill other human beings. In certain circumstances, the theory says, it is justified, that is, it is moral, to kill another human being. The emphasis is not on the universal command, "Thou shalt not kill," but on the circumstances of the particular situation which determine whether a killing is moral or immoral.

There is, one might say, no morality other than situational morality – a morality that takes into account all of the circumstances before making a determination about the quality of an act.

The central rule of morality for the community of faithful believers springs out of that community's fundamental experience of the union of God with all things in the universe, and its understanding of the ongoing development of that universe. In an evolving world, all things are carriers of the future. The more possibilities there are, the greater the chance for the one possibility that carries some significant development to spring into actuality. The first rule of action is, like the ancient Greek command to physicians, do no harm. The second is similar: promote to the fullest extent possible the development of all things. Preservation and promotion of life thus must be at the heart of the faithful community's moral rules.

But it is a matter of the preservation and promotion of all life, not just the life of a particular being or species. And there lies the source of all the interesting moral questions. Conflicting claims arise. At its simplest, two beings each require a certain thing; who rightly gets it?

Moral rules can only go so far in resolving real moral dilemmas – the situations in which real needs and claims are in conflict, and where each side in the conflict has a moral rule on which it relies. The modern issue of abortion is so difficult to resolve because there is, on one hand, the claim of the unborn fetus to life and, on the other hand, the claim of the woman to control of her own life. That latter claim is one only recently recognized (and still not acknowledged by many), but, like the recognition of the full humanity of slaves, it is propelling the debate about the morality of abortion into new territory. Looked upon simply as the killing of a fetus, *with no other part of the situation taken into account*, it is not so difficult to see that abortion is wrong. But take into account the mother's needs, claims and rights, as one must if the best action in the total situation and circumstances is to be determined, and a different debate emerges.

Few would hesitate, I think, to say that one human being should not be forced to give up a kidney or a lung to keep another human being alive, even if that other human being will surely die without that particular kidney or lung. Why is it then so easy for some to say a woman must always, in any and every situation, give up a part of her body for the benefit of the fetus? Would it be all right to require the taking of a lung or a kidney, if you got it back in nine months? To say that abortion is always right or always wrong is to give up half the problem by making absolute either the needs of the fetus or the needs of the woman. Recognizing both needs means recognizing that each is limited, neither is absolute. And that recognition takes us down into the cloudy realm of the individual decision and act.

True moral questions do not lend themselves to easy resolution. Rules are good and helpful, not in the sense that they determine the outcome of every situation, but because they tell us what are the important parts of the situation. You can't ignore the fetus, but neither can you ignore the woman. And then there are the needs and claims of the larger community. If we are faithful believers, we can't set aside or ignore even a single part of the universe in which we find ourselves.

And there are no substitutes for the individual making the decision. All societies make choices and formulate laws which its members are required to obey or pay the penalty for disobedience, regardless of what each member may think about the usefulness of a particular law. The difference between social laws and moral laws is that each individual makes the decision in the moral area. And the decision is not necessarily wrong just because it goes against a particular moral rule. It is wrong – "sinful" – only when the individual making the decision deliberately turns aside from all the circumstances involved in a particular act. No one on the outside can make a decision for the individual performing the act, nor are they able to judge whether the decision was right or wrong. Only the individual and God know – and they don't need to tell.

So, there are moral rules, lots of them. And they have a use. But they are only helpers, not the ultimate decision makers. When push comes to shove, as it always does, we each have to make our own decisions. "Mother, I'd rather do it myself" is not just a wish. It's the only way of living a moral life.

A Final Word on Comfort

Life as a faithful believer in a community of faithful believers is not always comfortable. If it is, it's probably a sign that you have traded your rightful bed of straw for the glitz and comfort of some resort where nothing is real except the bill at the end.

Cockroaches have been around for millions of years. They're successful survivors, but they are also evolutionary dead ends. They haven't died out and maybe they will be with us forever, but they aren't going anywhere either. Moving on involves being uncomfortable right now. Why else try for anything better if the present is everything you could want or imagine?

Not to worry. Simply being faithful to your deepest experience will make you as uncomfortable as you need to be. Just open your eyes and ears and let it happen. The universe, as someone has said, may be the ultimate free lunch. But like a picnic on a windy beach, it has lots of sand in it.

Chapter Eight

Postscript

I pass with relief from the tossing sea of Cause and Theory to the firm ground of Result and Fact.
– Winston Churchill, *The Malakand Field Force*

I myself believe that the evidence for God lies primarily in inner personal experiences.
– William James, *Pragmatism*

From the time I was about four until I was eight or nine, I had a recurring dream in which I identified myself with a large copper penny rolling rapidly across sand dunes until it came to a wooden structure that looked like an oil derrick. As the penny rolled under the four legs of the derrick, the structure suddenly would collapse and, as I looked upwards, huge beams were hurtling down upon me. I would awaken at this point in the dream, crying. When my mother came, I would tell her I had the bad dream again and she would explain that I must have eaten something that upset my stomach. She gave me a glass half full of water, with a small amount of bicarbonate of soda and I would go back to sleep, still fearful but reassured.

A year or two ago the dream came again. Only this time the derrick did not collapse and the penny rolled out the other side. I woke with a wonderful feeling of lightness and relief.

Results

Years ago I read a story about the first Chevrolet produced after the end of the Second World War. At a press conference announcing the new model, the president of Chevrolet talked at length about how marvelous the new car was, how improved over prewar models. He closed with the statement that Chevrolet was already working on the following year's model, which would have one small improvement over the present model. Inevitably asked what that improvement would be, he said: "A little sling under the engine to catch all the damn parts that keep falling out!"

I feel that way at least a little bit about this book. There are doubtless more parts falling out of the engine than I am even aware. So there is plenty of room for improvements, at least some of which I hope I will have the chance to make in coming years. Nonetheless, I have a great feeling of relief. No Everest has been scaled, but there is some sense of accomplishment. I have, I think, exorcised some of the demons by getting thoughts accumulating over the past 20 or 30 years onto paper. I can take a look at them in the light of day.

Part of the relief is simply from coming to the end of a task. But a larger part of it comes from a confirmation of what I have been coming to believe in bits and pieces, but always with a concern that those bits and pieces of belief make no sense at all. The ideas that appear in the previous chapters are no final system, as I hope I have made clear throughout the book. They are simply my current stopping place on a continuing journey. I expect there will be changes and additions and deletions as long as I live and continue to learn.

Some things, however, are likely to remain for the rest of the journey. I am, for instance, more than ever convinced that all genuine religious experience must begin in our inner depths. Faith is not a lesson we learn, as a set of rules and instructions in school. The starting point for all religious journeys is an experience of the real world about us that challenges and shatters all cursory views and explanations. There is a revelation of the depths of reality, along with, I think, some experienced sense of a ground that is present in the experience but that transcends that experience without being totally apart from it. It is the experience of myself and the world and God all held together in an enduring moment.

Further, I am convinced that out of that experience we build our religious systems of belief, attempting to find ways in which to talk about it and understand it and, to the extent possible, recreate it from time to time. We build those systems out of the material at hand – the language and ideas and symbols that we have come to know in the course of our daily lives. So every age and place puts it together in a somewhat different way. If we live in a thought world of political authoritarianism, static economics and unchanging structures of life, we will create a religious thought world like that of traditional Christianity. If we live in a world of political democracy, dynamic economics, continuing evolution and quantum indeterminacy, we will create a pattern of religious thought quite different.

The matter of judging the results remains with me. Are the ideas offered in this book any better than the ones I suggest they replace? How is it possible to tell whether new ideas have any greater validity than the ones of preceding generations? Might it not be best, after all, to stick with what has been tried and more or less worked for two millennia?

Well, I don't think sticking with the past is any longer possible. To do so is to become increasingly isolated, so that Christianity would be reduced to a sect and then finally to a quaint remnant of a prior age, something like alchemy. We cannot long avoid the task of putting together a new world of religious ideas if we are serious about a desire both to preserve Christianity and to understand and explain the Christian experience in a language

that also takes account of our contemporary understanding of the world around us.

There is no shortage of new ideas. The topic is hot
enough that it made the cover of a national newsmagazine
(*Newsweek*) while I was writing the final chapters of this
book. Inevitably the ideas are all over the patch, and some
discrimination is useful in determining which might have
at least a limited validity and which should be looked at
and then consigned to the scrap heap of "nice tries, but."
The following guidelines seem to me helpful in making
those necessary discriminations between valid and invalid
ideas.

1. Faith is the master of ideas.

The ideas are generated in order to assist us to
understand, talk about and recreate our fundamental
faith experiences. The ideas can have their own beauty
and they can easily lead us astray. But the determining
question must always be whether the ideas have a validity
based on their capacity to provide a mental picture of the
underlying experience. A good idea has an immediate
quality of fitting what it offers to explain. Like the everyday
experience of trying to think of a name or a thought that
temporarily eludes us, we know at once that we have come
upon the right idea when it finally rolls off our tongue.
Anything else is like the emperor's new clothes, which we
will see as nonexistent whenever we are open to look at
our experience with the eyes of a child.

2. Look for consistency.

The left brain isn't all bad. It has its uses, chief
among which is an insistence on the logical coherence
and consistency of ideas. The new world of ideas has to
be a *world,* which means that its parts must be coherently
related to each other. Not easily come by, or we would
not have to listen to people at once insisting upon the
death penalty while railing against abortion, or watch

parades of supporters of whales, seals, spotted owls and snail darters who yet have no time for the destitute and forlorn of the human species.

A starting point for this book was the thought that an understanding of the world as evolving, with some real indeterminacy in its basic structure, was fundamentally inconsistent with the idea of an unchanging God. The ideas of creator and creation ought, it seemed to me, have some coherence and consistency. So, also, should our understanding of human beings and our treatment of one another in our communities.

The search for consistency is rooted in the faith experience that the world is meaningful, that all things are in union with each other and with an underlying ground of being. When ideas spring forth in our consciousness and are found to be inconsistent with each other, we can be sure that one or all of the ideas are not valid expressions of underlying faith.

3. By their results shall you know them.

Ideas inevitably lead to action. As indicated in earlier chapters, one of the indications that something has been wrong with the traditional Christian set of ideas was the fact that these ideas have led Christians into spasms of judgment and persecution of their neighbors. There is something fundamentally wrong when a religion professedly based on the law of love (and, at a deeper level, on the experience of the uniting power of the ground of all being) engages in religious wars and hatred and condemnation of all peoples whose beliefs appear to differ.

Open Territories

A lot has been left unsaid and undone. For instance, I am now 60 years old, a time when it might be natural to say something of death and the Christian tradition of an afterlife. I recall the words of an 80-year-old aunt: "I don't feel old, but then I look down and see my mother's hands." So I suppose death is something I need to think about and incorporate into my understanding of myself, the world and God. All I can say in defense of this neglect is that I am too excited about participating in reality as it surrounds me here and now to spend time thinking about my end. Doubtless that will come in time – both the end and thoughts about it!

Another area of neglect is that of appropriate and valid forms of worship. Christian churches make much of the gathering for worship and devotion and yet I have said little or nothing about how the Christian community of the future would express itself in this way. My own church of origin has been heavily into liturgy, with the centuries old celebration of the Mass at the very heart of its life of worship and devotion. There is doubtless a good instinct here – the fundamental desire to celebrate in common that which is close to the heart of the faith of the community.

I don't know yet what kind of worship and devotion would be appropriate in a new world of beliefs, but I do know that I would like to see something closer to what I imagine must have been the gatherings of Jesus and his followers. The celebration of the Mass has become so stylized that, as a friend once put it, it is not just a question of believing that the bread and wine are the body and blood of Jesus Christ, it is now a question of believing that the wafers used as bread are really bread! Perhaps we could begin by periodically celebrating our unity and common faith with a meal that is really a meal. And it might be done in our homes for the most part, reserving the architectural monuments of the past to the occasional holiday celebration. Like Scarlett O'Hara, I'll have to think about that tomorrow.

Perhaps the greatest unfilled space in this book is some development of thought about the environment and ecology. As it should, I think, be clear, I do not see the human world as qualitatively different from the rest of creation. Human beings are simply part of an evolving process, tied heart and soul into that process. We stand in relation to all things, animal, vegetable and mineral, just as we stand also in relation to the machines we ourselves are in the process of creating.

Towards the end of writing this book, I came across Thomas Berry's *Befriending the Earth*, a book where the author discusses his profound insight into the changes in Christian thinking that must occur with our contemporary grasp of what it means to be a part of a process billions of years old. We live in holy space and holy time, and that space and time must be understood, respected and loved if we are to be ourselves, be what we ought to be. Berry's ideas are ones which, for me, pass the tests for determining the validity of ideas.

Doubtless there are many other areas that could or should have been discussed. But I have only been on the train of creation for an absurdly short time, and I have been thinking about it for a much shorter time still. I look to the future to help rectify some of the lacks and inconsistencies. The journey continues and, with good fortune, I will have other opportunities to develop and correct what has been said here, and to work with others in the process of creating the future.

I do not think John Donne got it quite right when he said that no man was an island, that we are all part of the mainland. We are all islands, quanta of energy in the sea of creation. But we have the opportunity placed before us to transcend our limits and connect with one another. It is our birthright, if we are only open to it, to walk on water.

Further Reading

The list of books provided below is not an effort to give a comprehensive listing of all the readings that influenced me in the writing of *Broken Rainbows*. It contains only a selection of readings that I think of as particularly significant, and that may lead the interested reader along the path that I followed. Many of the books contain extensive bibliographies and thus allow for one thing leading to another, much in the way my own thoughts developed.

Berger, Peter. *A Rumor of Angels: Modern Society and the Rediscovery of the Supernatural.* New York: Doubleday, 1990.

Berger, Peter. *The Sacred Canopy: Elements of a Sociological Theory of Religion.* Garden City, New York: Doubleday, 1969.

Berger, Peter and Luckman, Thomas. *The Social Construction of Reality.* Garden City, New York: Doubleday, 1966.

Berry, Thomas, C.P., with Clarke, Thomas, S.J. *Befriending the Earth: A Theology of Reconciliation Between Humans and the Earth.* Mystic, Connecticut: Twenty-Third Publications, 1992.

Boslough, John. *Masters of Time: Cosmology at the End of Innocence.* Reading, Massachusetts: Addison-Wesley, 1992.

Campbell, Joseph, ed. by Phil Cousineau. *The Hero's Journey: Joseph Campbell on His Life and Work.* San Francisco: Harper, 1990.

Campbell, Joseph. *The Inner Reaches of Outer Space: Metaphor as Myth and as Religion.* New York: Harper & Row, 1986.

Campbell, Joseph. *Myths to Live By.* New York: Bantam, 1973.

Campbell, Joseph, edited by John M. Maher and Dennie Briggs. *An Open Life: Joseph Campbell in Conversation with Michael Toms.* New York: Harper & Row, 1990.

Campbell, Joseph. *Transformations of Myth Through Time.* New York: Harper & Row, 1990.

Capra, Fritjof. *The Tao of Physics: An Exploration of the Parallels Between Modern Physics and Eastern Mysticism.* Boston: Shambhala, 1991.

Cohen, Jack and Stewart, Ian. *The Collapse of Chaos: Discovering Simplicity in a Complex World.* New York: Viking, 1994.

Crossan, John Dominic. *The Historical Jesus: The Life of a Mediterranean Jewish Peasant.* San Francisco: Harper, 1991.

Crossan, John Dominic. *Jesus: A Revolutionary Biography.* San Francisco: Harper, 1994.

Csikszentmihalyi, Mihaly. *The Evolving Self: A Pyschology for the Third Millenium.* New York: Harper Collins, 1993.

Csikszentmihalyi, Mihaly. *Flow: The Psychology of Optimal Experience.* New York: Harper, 1990.

Davies, Paul. *God and the New Physics.* New York: Simon & Schuster, 1983.

Dawkins, Richard. *The Blind Watchmaker: Why the Evidence of Evolution Reveals a Universe Without Design.* New York: W. W. Norton, 1987.

Fields, Rick, with Peggy Taylor, Rex Weyler and Rick Ingrasci. *Chop Wood, Carry Water: A Guide to Finding Spiritual Fulfillment in Everyday Life.* Los Angeles: Jeremy P. Tarcher, 1984.

Gleick, James. *Chaos: Making a New Science.* New York: Penguin, 1987.

Gleick, James. *Genius: The Life and Science of Richard Feynman.* New York: Vintage, 1993.

Gribbin, John. *In Search of Schrodinger's Cat: Quantum Physics and Reality.* Toronto: Bantam, 1984.

Harvey, Andrew. *Hidden Journey: A Spiritual Awakening.* New York: Henry Holt, 1991.

Hawking, Stephen. *A Brief History of Time: From the Big Bang to Black Holes.* New York: Bantam, 1988.

Jung, C. G., edited by Aniela Jaffe. *Memories, Dreams, Reflections.* New York: Vintage, 1989.

Keen, Sam. *Hymns to an Unknown God: Awakening the Spirit in Everyday Life.* New York: Bantam, 1994.

Kuhn, Thomas S. *The Structure of Scientific Revolutions.* Chicago: University of Chicago, 1962.

Kushi, Michio and Jack, Alex. *The Gospel of Peace: Jesus' Teaching of Eternal Truth.* Tokyo: Japan Publications, 1992.

Lederman, Leon, with Dick Teresi. *The God Particle: If the Universe is the Answer, What Is the Question?* Boston: Houghton Mifflin, 1993.

Manchester, William. *A World Lit Only by Fire: The Medieval Mind and the Renaissance.* Boston: Little, Brown, 1992.

Merzel, Dennis Genpo. *The Eye Never Sleeps: Striking to the Heart of Zen.* Boston: Shambhala, 1991.

Mitchell, Stephen. *Tao Te Ching.* New York: Harper, 1988.

Moore, Thomas. *Care of the Soul: A Guide for Cultivating Depth and Sacredness in Everyday Life.* New York: Harper, 1992.

Moss, Richard. *Black Butterfly: An Invitation to Radical Aliveness*. Berkeley, California: Celestial Arts: 1986.

Norris, Kathleen. *Dakota: A Spiritual Geography*. Boston: Houghton Mifflin, 1993.

Russell, Peter. *The White Hole in Time: Our Future Evolution and the Meaning of Now*. San Francisco: Harper, 1992.

Sagan, Carl and Druyan, Ann. *Shadows of Forgotten Ancestors: A Search for Who We Are*. New York: Random House, 1992.

Suzuki, Shunryu, edited by Trudy Dixon. *Zen Mind, Beginner's Mind*. New York: Weatherhill, 1970.

Teilhard de Chardin, Pierre. *The Divine Milieu*. New York: Harper & Brothers, 1960.

Teilhard de Chardin, Pierre. *The Phenomenon of Man*. New York: Harper & Brothers, 1959.

Waldrop, M. Mitchell. *Complexity: The Emerging Science at the Edge of Order and Chaos*. New York: Touchstone, 1992.

Watts, Alan. *The Way of Liberation*. New York: Weatherhill, 1983.

Watts, Alan. *The Way of Zen*. New York: Vintage. 1989.

Wills, Christopher. *The Wisdom of the Genes: New Pathways in Evolution*. New York: Basic Books, 1989.

Zohar, Danah and Marshall, Ian. *The Quantum Society: Mind, Physics and a New Social Vision*. New York: William Morrow, 1994.

Zukav, Gary. *The Dancing Wu Li Masters: An Overview of the New Physics*. New York: Morrow Quill, 1979.